Relationships are a central component to the human experience. Whether we feel their absence, struggle to maintain them, or find love in the peace they provide, relationships are the source of our greatest joys and greatest wounds. It is no wonder, then, to discover that "relationship" has its origins in the very nature and heart of God. Jeanne models God's relational heart, and you will hear her heart (for you specifically) in the pages of this book. May God use her words to inspire and challenge you to respond to God's invitation to be fully known, entirely forgiven, and perfectly loved.

—Rev. Rielly McLaren
Community Chaplain for Federal Ex-Offenders,
Windsor, Ontario

THE
Family Tree

God Gets
His Family Back

Jeanne Best

THE FAMILY TREE
Copyright © 2018 by Jeanne Best

Printed in Canada

ISBN: 978-1-4866-1760-9

Word Alive Press
119 De Baets Street Winnipeg, MB R2J 3R9
www.wordalivepress.ca

Cataloguing in Publication information can be obtained from Library and Archives Canada.

To Marcia,
my "spunky" younger sister
and dearest friend.

Acknowledgements

I THANK MY HEAVENLY FATHER, WHO KNOWS ME AND LOVES ME AND ENCOURAGES ME TO try less and surrender more.

I thank the Women of Hope at Hope City Church in Barrie, Ontario, for giving me the opportunity to teach what God lays on my heart. Your lives, your challenges, and your questions inspire me.

I thank my friends and family, who were willing to read and share their thoughts and support me in this work.

CONTENTS

Introduction

THE SEED THAT GREW INTO *THE FAMILY TREE* WAS PLANTED ABOUT TEN YEARS AGO. IT all began when my mother asked me to pick up a book at our local Christian bookstore. Being the "book" person that I am, I just had to *carefully* read it before I delivered it. Andrew Farley's book *The Naked Gospel* challenged my thinking as nothing else had for a long time. The question that most captured my attention was this: "If Jesus died once for all and shed His blood to pay the debt of man's sin, why do we keep asking God to forgive us?"[1] That one question opened a door for me and gave me permission to look carefully at what I believed.

Looking back, I was reminded that a lot had changed over the years. Sermons about God's wrath and the reality of hell had been replaced by sermons about God's love and His plan for our lives. Legalistic rules that restricted all manner of lifestyle choices had been rejected. Boundaries had disappeared. But teachings that rise from extreme positions often don't endure. This is the changing face of religion.

But God's truth doesn't change.

Even though we can't see God, I don't believe that Christian faith is blind faith. When I consider the intricacy of design and the coordination of systems in all the created things, I see a Master Designer who loves beauty and desires relationship with His creation. When I ponder the

---

[1] Andrew Farley, *The Naked Gospel* (Grand Rapids, MI: Zondervan, 2009), 136.

wonder of God's Word written by forty authors in three languages over fifteen hundred years, how can I doubt its truth? When I think about the hundreds of fulfilled prophecies concerning the tiny nation of Israel and Jesus, who was born of this family line, how can I not believe that there is salvation for those who believe in Jesus Christ? The only thing that's really constant in our changing world is the Word of God. It's my rock, my foundation. I knew that if I was going to find an answer to that question about forgiveness it was going to be in the Bible, not in the religious teachings of man.

My search led me to a renewed understanding of what the Bible teaches about forgiveness, and there were lots of surprises along the way. Even though most Christians are taught to ask God to forgive their sin, the apostle Paul in his letters to the churches never once instructs believers to follow this practice. I discovered how easy it is to misinterpret and misunderstand Scripture when we neglect to consider either the context of a particular verse or the greater historical context. Yes, God wants me to confess my sin, but He also wants me to be confident that the shed blood of Christ was a sufficient sacrifice for my sin. He wants me to praise and thank Him that my sin is forgiven.

Learning to live in the freedom of forgiveness changes you. It's so much easier to not be offended by the careless words of others and to let go of things that aren't important. Believing that I'm forgiven hasn't left me thinking that I can do whatever I want. Just the opposite. It has freed my soul, and the thanksgiving I feel has encouraged me to reach for greater heights of surrender and obedience to my Lord.

I love to teach others this truth, and recently, after she had attended several classes, a lady came up to me and said, "When you first started I wasn't sure I agreed with you, but what you've taught us about forgiveness really has changed my prayer time. Instead of feeling guilty and burdened by my sin, I spend more time thanking and praising God for the forgiveness that is mine in Christ. It's really made a difference in my relationship with God."

Our society today is biblically illiterate. We're drowning in Bibles that are rarely opened. We've lost our understanding of the gospel because we've neglected the Word of God. The technological world that we live in has changed the way we relate to one another, and when you combine these things it's our families that are suffering the consequences.

I'm troubled, as I see increasing numbers of broken families in our society and in our churches. Immorality and disorder are on the increase as the structure and stability of the family slip away. We've become distracted, indifferent, and self-absorbed. There is hope, but it will never be found in the changing rules of religion or by rewriting God's handbook on relationships. Andrew Farley reminded me to hold those things I believe in up against the Word of God, because if it's God's truth it will always reflect the glory of who He is and what He has done.

I write to remind people that God has a lot to say about life and family. In the end, our hope is in the person of Jesus Christ. He is the source of the renewal and restoration our families need. I pray that you, my readers, will open your minds and hearts to take a fresh look at that which never changes.

CHAPTER 1
For the Love Of…

I WAS HOOKED! THE TLC NETWORK SERIES *WHO DO YOU THINK YOU ARE?* HAD CAPTURED my attention and landed a faithful viewer. During each episode a guest celebrity went on a fascinating journey back in time to search out the amazing and sometimes notorious exploits of previous generations.

Information about our ancestors is more readily available now than ever before, and increasing numbers of people are exploring their family roots. There can be surprises for those who are brave enough to venture down this road, but whether we find leaders of distinction or rascals and rogues, we long to discover meaning and identity in these family connections. They're what make us unique and special.

The yearning of our hearts is to find personal significance, to know that we belong, to know that we are loved. We look to family first because we're all part of the collective human family. Family is the common cord that binds human beings together and connects us to God. In his book *Vanishing Grace,* journalist and author Philip Yancey shares the following personal insight:

> In my lifelong study of the Bible I have looked for an overarching theme, a summary statement of what the whole sprawling book

is about. I have settled on this: "God gets His family back." From the first book to the last the Bible tells of wayward children and the tortuous lengths to which God will go to bring them home. Indeed, the entire biblical drama ends with a huge family reunion in the book of Revelation.[2]

As Yancey suggests, there are a lot of twists and turns in this story. There are more plots and subplots than you can count. The story is told by over forty authors, writing in three different languages over a period of fifteen hundred years. Not only that, the story flows from the beginning of the book to its conclusion in a way that no human effort could ever achieve. Some might question whether this is a true story, but when you consider the sheer volume of manuscripts, the fulfilled prophecies, and the confirmation of archaeological findings, it's pretty hard to dispute the accuracy of the facts. The Bible is the story of God's family, and it gives more insight into the human condition than all the theories of man put together. It demonstrates a knowledge of human behaviour that only our Maker would have. God's Word is a handbook on relationships. It's an instruction manual on how family works, from the One who designed family.

FOR THE LOVE OF FAMILY

In the beginning, God (Father, Son and Holy Spirit) created. Each day of creation just got better and better. The beauty, the order, the design—it was all so incredibly breathtaking! The Creator was excited, and periodically He would exclaim, "It is good!" At one point the fellowship within (Father, Son, and Spirit) consulted with one another and said, *"Let Us make man in Our image."*[3] Man would be His crowning achievement, a personal being outside of Himself who would express His righteousness and holiness. And so Adam rose from the dust, the first created son, brought to life by the breath of the Spirit of God.

---

[2] Philip Yancey, *Vanishing Grace* (Grand Rapids, MI: Zondervan, 2014), 51.
[3] Genesis 1:26.

> God was pleased with man, but then He paused. Something wasn't quite right, and He said to Himself, *"It is not good that man should be alone; I will make him a helper comparable to him."*[4] And so God used Adam's own bone and flesh to create Eve, the first woman.
>
> Eve was similar to Adam, bones and flesh, hands and feet. But she was different, a softer, gentler creation. She would be a helper to Adam, as God Himself was a helper, and He took joy in enlarging the expression of Himself in Eve. He created them to complete one another.
>
> If Adam was the crowning achievement of creation, Eve was the jewel in that crown. The unity of love and respect within the Godhead would be lived out an earth through them. God looked at all He had created with satisfaction, and *"Indeed it was very good."*[5]

I've heard some jokingly say that creation is only described as "very good" after the creation of woman, but I believe Genesis 1:31 refers to the whole of creation, including the relationship of the first man and woman, the first family, and "*it*" was very good. That special union that God created between the first husband and wife was the promise of the fellowship that humans would share with God and with one another. Family would be a fellowship of love and belonging, a picture of God Himself. Relationships on earth would reflect relationships in heaven. God doesn't just *have* relationship; God *is* relationship, and His design for family was based on the template of Himself. It was out of the raw material of human creation that God designed family.

> Adam and Eve were made in the image and likeness of their Creator, and their job was to run the family business, which at that time was ruling the earth as their Creator's representative. But then the family had a falling out.

---

[4] Genesis 2:18.
[5] Genesis 1:31.

> Adam and Eve failed to follow the Lord's instructions. They were smart enough to accomplish great things but foolish enough to think they could do it on their own. They chose to disobey, and their disobedience gave entrance to sin and evil. It created such a rift that the children who would be born to them, as well as the generations that followed, would no longer be part of God's family.
>
> Adam and Eve's children would bear their fallen human likeness[6] rather than God's holy and righteous image. The relationship of love and trust that they had enjoyed with God was gone. The beauty of their world was destroyed, and the consequence of their sin was death.

This is how God lost His family.

The brokenness that we read about in the garden was just a shadow of things to come, and it pretty much reflects life as we know it today. It's easy for us to turn our backs on God's definitions of right and wrong because we think we know better. We sometimes have trouble getting along, and family is far from what God designed it to be.

In spite of all this, God wants His wayward, disobedient children back. He wants us to come home, and the reason He goes to such great lengths to bring us home is simply this: He loves us.

You are special to Him. God's love is impossible for humans to fully comprehend, but His love of family begins with His love for you.

FOR THE LOVE OF YOU

Have you ever wondered why God created you? God has no need of anything or anyone outside Himself, so what was the point of creating humans in the first place?

God isn't lonely. He is one in His being, and yet His divine essence exists in three forms: God the Father, God the Son, and God the Holy Spirit. Each person of the Godhead loves, honours, and glorifies the other, and within this relationship there is belonging, peace, and

---

[6] Genesis 5:3.

limitless enjoyment. God didn't need humans in order to experience love and belonging.

Jonathan Edwards, a nineteenth century preacher, said that the only reason God would have for creating us was not to *get* the cosmic joy of relationship (because He already had that) but to *share* it.[7] A friend of mine was recently talking about how she saw her children as an expression of herself. She could see herself in their talents and skills, in their looks and mannerisms. So it is with God. The God of the universe created you to be an expression of Himself. What an amazing thought that is!

> Alexander Tsiaras, an artist and mathematician, was working as an associate professor of medicine at Yale University when he participated in the production of a video called *Conception to Birth: Visualized.*[8] It's a high-speed journey through prenatal human development, a trip that leaves you wondering how anyone could doubt the existence of God. One of the marvels that Tsiaras highlights is the way that collagen cells differentiate during human development. Collagen is opaque everywhere throughout the body, except in the eye. In the cornea of the eye these rope-like building block cells take on a gridlike pattern, producing a clarity that allows us to see. Tsiaras is in awe of how collagen cells know to do this just in the eye. He also marvels at the way the body changes the rate of its development. If the rate of developmental change occurring at thirty-six days after conception remained constant, we would weigh 1.5 tons at birth. It's our DNA that contains all these necessary instructions, but the number and complexity of these processes is mind boggling. Tsiaras admits that these biological mechanisms at work within a single system are beyond his comprehension as a mathematician. His conclusion is that he has seen divinity at work.

---

[7] John E. Smith, Harry S. Stout, and Kenneth P. Minkema, eds., *Jonathan Edwards Reader* (New Haven, CT: Yale University Press, 2003).

[8] Visit ted.com and search "Divinity" to view a clip of the video.

The Bible describes humans as "fearfully and wonderfully made."[9] God's hands made you and formed you;[10] the hairs on your head are numbered;[11] and He determined the days of your life before you were born.[12] The longing of God's heart is for you to recognize that He is your Creator and to experience His love.

Before Jesus went to the cross He prayed, "*This is eternal life, that they may know You.*"[13] God reaches down from heaven to connect with you. He shows you His greatness, beauty, and power in creation. He whispers eternity into your heart, calling you and drawing you to Himself. You were created with a desire for God, and your heart has a space that only He can fill. St. Augustine said, "You [God] have made us for yourself, and our heart is restless until it rests in you."[14]

God's love for you doesn't depend on who you know or what others think or whether you feel worthy. It's a love that's based on the deliberate choice of the one who loves rather than the worthiness of the one who is loved. God chooses to love you, and all He really wants is for you to love Him back.

He could have programmed you to love Him, like a programmer programs a computer, but then it wouldn't be love. God created you with the ability to choose because He wants your love for Him to be a choice that you freely make. Love is not a duty or an obligation. Love is a choice, and without choice there is no love. "God loves us simply because of His choice, not because of anything in us (which may change), nor anything around us (which may change). He loves us because He loves us."[15] The door to the Kingdom is wide open, but only those who respond to God's love are able to enter in.

---

[9] Psalm 139:14.
[10] Psalm 119:73.
[11] Matthew 10:30.
[12] Psalm 139:16.
[13] John 17:3.
[14] Elizabeth Knowles, *The Oxford Dictionary of Quotations,* 5th ed. (New York, NY: Oxford University Press, 2001), 35.
[15] Timothy Keller, *Romans 8–16 for You* (n.p.: The Good Book Company, 2015), 54.

FOR THE LOVE OF THE SON

> Rick Hoyt was born with cerebral palsy, a condition that results when oxygen to the brain is cut off during birth. Rick's mind and thinking are normal, but he is unable to control his limbs and can only speak with the aid of a computer.
>
> When he was fifteen years old he asked his father, Dick, if he could run in a charity race to help a student lacrosse player who had been injured. This father-son team not only entered the race, they finished the five-mile course, coming in next to last, but not last. The rest is history. After competing in some 1,100 races, including 32 Boston Marathons, Team Hoyt announced that the 2014 Boston Marathon would be their last official father-son race.[16]

There are so many lessons to be drawn from this story, but perhaps what rises to the top is the incredible love of this father for his son. Dick's love for his son led him to make sacrifices. He was willing to suffer pain for the good of his son. He committed himself to the cause and persevered beyond all expectations. Dick freely chose to make these sacrifices because of love, and perhaps if there were more fathers like Dick we might catch a glimpse of the true meaning of love. Even so, Dick's love for his son still doesn't come close to God's love. I'm sure Dick would be the first to admit that he hasn't always been a perfect father.

All relationships have their ups and downs. Do you ever lack trust in relationships or impose higher standards on others than you do on yourself? Are there situations that make you angry or frustrated? If someone does something nice for you, do you wonder what they want in return? The potential list of shortfalls is long and varied, but the outcome leads us to the same place. Selfish behaviour has become all too common.

Those who don't know God assume that He's the same as we are and treat Him more like the guy next door than their Creator. Rather than

---

[16] See "Team Hoyt," Wikipedia, last modified June 14, 2018, 17:17, https://en.wikipedia.org/wiki/Team_Hoyt.

seeing that the love of earthly fathers (and mothers) falls short of God's love, we tend to see flawed human love as a reflection of God. When we create God in our image, we don't always like what we see.

But God isn't like us.

If we really knew and understood God as the wonderful Father He is, it would be easy to believe Him. God doesn't just *have* love; God *is* love, and when 1 Corinthians 13 describes love, it is describing God. Love is patient, kind, not envious or proud, not rude or self-seeking. God's love for you is selfless and unconditional. It seeks what is best for you regardless of who you are or what you've done. In his book *The Search for Significance*, Robert McGee suggests that we replace the word *love* in 1 Corinthians 13 with *my Father*.[17] This is the love that God has for all His children.

> My Father is very patient and kind.
> My Father is not envious, never boastful.
> My Father is not arrogant.
> My Father is never rude; nor is He self-seeking.
> My Father is not quick to take offense.
> My Father keeps no score of wrongs.
> My Father knows no limit to His endurance, no end to His trust.

It is this Father love that Jesus lives out before us in the Gospels as He paints a picture of the divine relationship between Father and Son. Jesus is the Son who submits Himself to the Father's will. He comes to earth to complete the work that the Father has given Him to do. He dies on a cross so that sinful human beings who were created in His image might be rescued from death, so that they might once again bear the family image.

Jesus' love of the Father and submission to the divine purpose led to His death and resurrection, but once the work was completed He took His place at the Father's right hand. Having defeated death, He is exalted and glorified.

---

[17] Robert McGee, "God's Answer: Reconciliation," chap. 6 in *The Search for Significance* (Nashville, TN: Thomas Nelson, 1998, 2003).

For this reason I bow my knees to the Father of our Lord Jesus Christ, from whom the whole family in heaven and earth is named, that He would grant you… to know the love of Christ which passes knowledge; that you may be filled with all the fullness of God.[18]

We view life from such a personal perspective today. I challenge you to step away from that mindset and view life on earth from God's eternal perspective. Exploring ancestral connections and family roots is interesting, but our true significance and belonging transcends life on earth. We were created for an eternal purpose, but the tighter we hang on to the things of this world, the more we lose our grip on what this means. "The great God of heaven set his love upon you in the depths of eternity before time, and is now working out his plan to live with you forever in eternity."[19] What God does, He does for the love of the Son, and what He does for the love of the Son… *He does for the love of you.*

---

[18] Ephesians 3:14–19.
[19] Keller, *Romans 8–16 for You*, 54.

CHAPTER 2
Understanding the Father

YOUR LIFE EXPERIENCES, YOUR GENES, AND YOUR CULTURAL VALUES ALL SHAPE THE unique way that you define the world around you. All these factors meld together, making you the one-of-a-kind person you are. Today it's popular to call this your worldview. Everything that you believe to be true about life hangs on this framework. It drives all your thoughts, feelings, decisions, and actions. It's your perspective. It's simply the way you view things.

"Hand me my glasses, please." My husband, Jim, and I had just left the dock and set out for a few days of vacation on our small cabin cruiser. I was down below in the cabin, putting things away. Jim was standing on the deck, looking down at me. After a quick scan I asked, "Where are they?"

"Right there," he said, with pointing finger.

With just a hint of frustration I said, "I don't see any glasses," and then with just a hint of impatience Jim repeated, "They're right there."

I stepped closer to the counter, and as I started moving things I saw that the elusive glasses, clearly in Jim's line of view from above, had been hidden from my view by a tea towel.

Having a different perspective when looking for glasses is not that important in the big scheme of things, but trying to understand life from a different perspective than God's can affect both the way we live our lives and the quality of life that we experience. Have you ever taken time to think about God's perspective on life? What's His view of family and the world today? What was His eternal perspective in the beginning when He first created man?

Lots of things happen in life that we don't like and we don't understand, things that can cause us to question the love and goodness of God. Do you sometimes wonder where God is coming from? Does He see you? Does He hear you? Perhaps it's time to step up to the counter, move things around, and take another look.

GOD'S PURPOSE

God created humans to expand the expression of Himself in the universe. He didn't give Adam a complex human body with an empty mind. God made flesh-and-blood people with a knowledge of their Creator.

God created people for relationship. The Son walked with Adam and Eve in the garden. The Holy Spirit filled their minds and hearts with wisdom and love. Adam and Eve were the object of the Father's love. *"Behold what manner of love the Father has bestowed on us, that we should be called children of God!"* [20]

But relationship was never meant to be an end in itself. Rather, it was the means to a greater and more glorious purpose. It was to the first human family that the Father delegated divine authority over earth. God rules the universe from the highest heaven, a kingdom invisible to our eyes. He established a visible kingdom on earth and created man in order to extend His heavenly rulership. He is a Father who wants to have a loving relationship with His children, but He is also the King who must have the allegiance of the citizens of His kingdom.

---

[20] 1 John 3:1.

Every year when November rolls around there's usually something in the media that brings to mind the 1963 assassination of President John F. Kennedy. One of those memories is the picture of a three-year-old boy, John Jr., standing at attention as he salutes the passing casket of the president, his daddy.

But there's another picture that we also remember with vivid emotion: the picture of that same little boy playing under his daddy's desk in the oval office, the desk of the president of the United States. John Jr. was both son and citizen, and in these relationships we see a beautiful picture of love and submission embracing one another. The boy knew his father with an intimate affection and yet respected the position he held and acknowledged his headship.

When Adam and Eve ate the forbidden fruit in the garden, they weren't just disobeying their Father; they were betraying the King of heaven and the responsibility of rulership that He had entrusted to them. God was their Father, but He was also their sovereign head, and in disobeying the King's decree they were disloyal to both the King and the Kingdom. It was an act of treason, a crime for which death is the penalty. The spiritual unity between God and man lay shattered and in pieces around the roots of the tree of the knowledge of good and evil, a tree that led to death.

Satan had deceived the children of the King and was pleased with his accomplishment. There would be no glorious Kingdom. He was in charge now and would see to it that these human creatures suffered and blamed their Father for the mess they were now in. Satan had driven a wedge between God and His children. There would be no loving family.

But there is another tree. It is the cross of Calvary, the place where man would be redeemed through the death of Jesus Christ and where all the requirements of the King's law would be fulfilled.[21] As the agony of the cross lay before Him, Jesus said, "*The hour has come that the Son*

---

[21] Romans 8:3–4.

of Man should be glorified… for this purpose I came to this hour. Father, glorify Your name."[22] Obviously there was a lot that Satan didn't know about God!

God's purpose from the beginning has always been to reveal the glory of who He is, the sovereign Lord and loving Father. Here's what God says about His purpose: "*Declaring the end from the beginning, and from ancient times things that are not yet done… 'My counsel shall stand'… I have spoken it: I will also bring it to pass. I have purposed it; I will also do it.*"[23]

GOD'S PLAN

God's plan was never about revenge. It's a plan that simply puts things back the way they were intended to be. As the drama of spiritual conflict rages around us, the battle is being fought on two fronts: the loyalty of our hearts to the Father, and the submission of our wills to the King.

When God gave human beings freedom of choice, man's rejection and disloyalty became real possibilities. The potential for sin and evil was always there. It was the cost of creating sons and daughters, and it was a risk that God was willing to take.

> One of the things that makes humans intelligent beings is freedom. They had the freedom to obey God or to turn away from Him. And to turn away from God, the source of all goodness, is to create evil. Evil does not have an independent existence, nor was it created by God. Evil is created by sin.[24]

When Adam chose to operate outside the bounds of the knowledge God had given him, it created havoc, but God never goes back on His word. From then on the consequences of human choice had to be factored into His plan. Freedom comes with a high price tag.

> One of the basic freedoms we enjoy is the right to make our own decisions, and inherent in the right to make decisions

---

[22] John 12:23–28.

[23] Isaiah 46:10–11.

[24] Charles Colson, *The Problem of Evil* (Wheaton, IL: Tyndale House, 1999), 102.

is the right to make good or bad decisions. Years ago when I worked in community health, we would occasionally receive calls from concerned individuals who were worried about the welfare of someone in their family or community. They wanted someone "in authority" to step in and fix the problem, but that wasn't always possible. Sometimes people, like George, didn't want help.

George was an elderly man who rented a room in a boarding home. His landlord called to report that George was losing weight and his room was a mess of hoarded garbage. We visited George, but he didn't want anything to do with us. George had rights, and without his consent, and with no power of attorney representing him, we had to step back. Nothing could be done at that point. Unfortunately, George became very ill before he acknowledged his need.

God is the King, and His Kingdom operates within a legal framework. He gave man the legal authority to act as His representative on earth and then stepped back, allowing man to use that authority. He would not arbitrarily intervene in the affairs of men, but rather He would enter into agreements, or covenants, as they're called in the Bible. God's covenants with man spell out the terms of their relationship and their obligations to one another.

The first part of the Bible records a covenant between God and Israel in which God entrusts the Israelites with His law.[25] These ten commandments were the constitution of the Kingdom, and they were literally carved in stone! In exchange for their obedience God promised to bless the people of Israel with health, protection, and prosperity.[26] But the covenant didn't work. Men insisted on doing things their own way[27] and continued to be deceived by evil. They rejected God's law and worshipped idols. They broke the covenant by turning away from God, and so a new covenant became necessary.

---

[25] Exodus 20, 24:3.
[26] Deuteronomy 7:12–16.
[27] Judges 21:25.

Andrew Murray, a nineteenth century theologian, explains it this way:

> The reason for there being two covenants is to be found in the need of giving the Divine will and the human will, each their due place in the working out of man's destiny. God ever takes the initiative. Man must have the opportunity to do his part, and to prove either what he can do, or needs to have done for him.[28]

The old covenant (law) was insufficient to save man and bring about his reconciliation with God because man wasn't able to do his part. But at the same time the old covenant was indispensable to the working of God's plan because it revealed God's standard and man's inability to meet that standard. It showed man's helplessness to save himself. It showed man's hopelessness. God had to enter humanity and do for man what man could not do for himself. God, in the person of His Son, provided the human co-operation that was needed in order to save humanity from eternal death. He spoke it and will bring it to pass. He purposed it, and He will do it. This has always been God's plan.

GOD'S PERSPECTIVE

It must have seemed like any chance God had of fulfilling His purpose was destroyed when the first human family betrayed Him, but the thought of just giving it all up to Satan and walking away never crossed His mind. The annihilation of creation was never a consideration. God had a very different perspective.

In *The Serpent of Paradise*, Erwin Lutzer describes God's response to Satan's invasion of creation this way:

> God decided to use Lucifer… to demonstrate truths that would have been permanently hidden if evil had not entered the

---

[28] Andrew Murray, *The Two Covenants* (Fort Washington, PA: Christian Literature Crusade, 1995), 18.

universe. The curtain would rise on a drama acted out on earth in which Lucifer and God, justice and good and evil, would be in conflict.[29]

The opening act of this drama must have seemed pretty bleak to Adam and Eve. Sin and evil were unleashed and tore through creation with the destructive force of an F10 tornado. The curse of death lay like a cold, wet blanket over all creation, transforming both man and his world. Immortal human bodies became frail flesh that would die and return to the dust of a cursed ground. The breathtaking beauty and greatness of nature became a shadow of the original glory and majesty God created it to display. Nature's energy began to wind down, caught up in cycles of death, decay, and efforts to re-establish itself. Ecosystems that once operated in perfect harmony were now out of sync, and nature continues to bear the weight of this frustration. "*The whole creation groans*"[30] as it waits to be "*delivered from the bondage of corruption.*"[31]

Fortunately, God doesn't operate within the bounds of time and space. God is eternal and has an eternal perspective. The plan to accomplish His purpose was carefully devised before the earth was created. Jesus was with God in the beginning. He is the Lamb of God, slain before the foundation of the world.[32]

It was a rescue operation unlike any the world had ever seen. It was planned in eternity, and the Old Testament prophets announced it to the world. "*Unto us a Child is born, unto us a Son is given.*"[33]

Hundreds of years later, "*when the fullness of the time had come, God sent forth His Son, born of a woman, born under the law.*"[34] Jesus knew only too well what His mission was. "*God so loved the world that He gave His only*

---

[29] Erwin Lutzer, *The Serpent of Paradise* (Chicago, IL: Moody Press, 196), 37.
[30] Romans 8:22.
[31] Romans 8:21.
[32] Revelation 13:8.
[33] Isaiah 9:6.
[34] Galatians 4:4.

begotten Son."[35] The objective of the "op" was to infiltrate planet Earth and buy back humanity out of the slave market of sin. The cost of this purchase would be His lifeblood, and the immensity of what lay ahead weighed heavy on Him. It would take a power beyond His humanity to endure the rejection and the brutality, but it was the thought of what lay beyond the grave that kept Him going, and He was ready.

"Father, the hour has come. Glorify Your Son, that Your Son may also glorify You... I have glorified You on the earth. I have finished the work which You have given Me to do. And now, O Father, glorify Me together with Yourself, with the glory which I had with You before the world was."[36]

Legally, God accomplished His purpose at the cross, but experientially, the full glory of it is yet to come. This is somewhat similar to when a person wins their case in court and receives a judgment in their favour. Legally, they've won, but the benefits of their victory are yet to be realized. Those who believe in Christ are forgiven and receive the gift of eternal life here and now, but they are still clothed in frail flesh. One day they will shed mortality and be clothed in a body that will live forever without decay or corruption.[37]

The world we live in also waits with eager expectation for deliverance from its bondage to decay, a deliverance that will be *"into the glorious liberty of the children of God."*[38] God has spoken it and will bring it to pass.

God justly condemned the rebellion against Himself and His Kingdom and in so doing showed Himself to be a God of wrath. God's wrath is His reaction to all that contradicts His righteousness and holiness. It is not an out-of-control bad temper that flares in response to wounded pride. God's wrath is a necessary part of His moral perfection because God alone, as Creator, determines what is right and what is wrong.

---

[35] John 3:16.
[36] John 17:1–5.
[37] Romans 8:23.
[38] Romans 8:21.

God cannot ignore sin and evil, because the penalty for rebellion against the King and His Kingdom is death.[39] If He turned a blind eye and failed to judge sin, then He would be neither just nor righteous. God's wrath shows Him to be a King who demonstrates righteousness in His character and justice in His rulership, but He views us with compassion because He is our Maker. By promising a Saviour, He demonstrated the truth of His love and His mercy. Love and judgment are perfectly balanced in a just and merciful God.

God's eternal perspective never changes, because He never changes.[40] Sin and evil will ultimately be destroyed. Goodness and righteousness will prevail. This is the glory of who He is. As He planned it before time began, so it will be. His family will be restored. His will *will* be done on earth as it is in heaven.

The cross of Calvary is the family tree of the children of God, and Jesus is the firstborn among many brothers.[41] God is restoring wholeness and uniting all things in Christ. Those who believe in Him experience His presence now and will one day share in His inheritance.[42] Until then, God is still at work. He is both loving Father and sovereign King. His end game is the extension of His Kingdom on earth, where His children will reign in the glory of a new creation,[43] a place where all will acknowledge that Jesus is King of kings and Lord of lords,[44] to the glory of God the Father.

This is the framework on which God hangs eternity. This is God's perspective... *And this is the story of the family tree.*

---

[39] Romans 6:23.
[40] Malachi 3:6.
[41] Romans 8:29.
[42] Romans 8:17.
[43] Revelation 5:9–10.
[44] Revelation 17:14.

CHAPTER 3
A Family With History

DO YOU REMEMBER THINKING ABOUT THE BIG QUESTIONS WHEN YOU WERE YOUNG? WHAT does God look like? How can God be everywhere at once? Even today I find it difficult to comprehend the vastness of the universe or to measure "forever" in my mind.

I remember thinking about all the people on earth and wondering if we might run out of space one day. I remember being taught about evolution and seeing that infamous chart that shows man evolving from an ape. It never made sense to me, because there was no provision for the reality of women in the world. Would the evolutionists really have me believe that my heritage was a pool of sludge?

Somehow deep inside I've always believed that God created man and woman and that if we traced the generations back in time there had to be a first man and a first woman. I wonder what life was like for them, living in a garden without any knowledge of sin and evil. What was it like to walk with God and know His presence? But then they disobeyed. I wonder what that was like.

Adam and Eve looked at each other with an intensity they had never known before. Beads of sweat formed on Adam's brow. Eve's hands trembled. Feelings welled up in them that they'd never experienced before: fear, worry, uncertainty. They had disobeyed their Creator, and in an instant everything changed. Their shame sickened them. Their guilt overwhelmed them. As surely as they had known good, they now knew evil.

The serpent stood by, bent over with laughter and ridicule. He had destroyed their allegiance to heaven's King. They had been deceived by the evil one, Satan. The incorruptible became corrupt. The immortal put on mortality, and the Holy Spirit of God withdrew. Death now reigned. Physically they looked the same, but just as a cut flower fades, withers, and dies, their bodies would now age, weaken, and return to dust.

Adam and Eve must have wondered how God would react to their rebellion, and their new knowledge of evil made them panic. They even tried to hide from God. I wonder what that was like. God had told them that they would die if they ate fruit from the tree of the knowledge of good and evil, but death was beyond their experience.

As the Holy Spirit withdrew His presence, the light of His life in them vanished, leaving behind a darkness in their minds and spirits. As their Creator slaughtered animals before them to provide a covering for their shame and nakedness, they learned that physical life is in the blood, and they were literally clothed with the consequences of their bad choice. Where there had been peace and joy, there was now pain and strife.

THE PROMISE IN THE GARDEN

As I reflect on the story of the fall of man, I'm amazed by the mercy and compassion of God. First of all, He showed up. He didn't abandon them. Yes, He judged their sin, because a righteous God must judge sin, but then right there in the midst of judgment He made an amazing promise. He announced that He had a plan to destroy the sin and evil that had now invaded His creation and that it would happen through the Seed of the woman. Sin brought death, but God promised that life would be restored. He gave His word that a human Saviour would destroy the evil one.

Right from the beginning God said that there would be a Messiah, a Deliverer. Right from the beginning we can see that the promise in the garden was all about Jesus. *"And this is the promise that He has promised us—eternal life."*[45] *"And this is the testimony: that God has given us eternal life, and this life is in His Son."*[46]

I believe that God equipped Adam and Eve with keen memories and the ability to record names and events, because they carried God's spoken promise out of the garden and passed it on to the generations that followed.

Genesis, the first book of the Old Testament, gives us the history of man's early days on earth. Genesis 5 is a genealogical record of Adam's descendants up to the time of Noah and the great flood. It lists specific names and lifespans, and there is nothing in it to indicate that it's anything but what it claims to be—a true and accurate record.

Adam lived 930 years and was still living when Noah's father, Lamech, was born. Isn't it interesting that Adam was alive to give an eyewitness testimony of God's promise to those in his family line who believed God? No doubt Lamech had heard the stories of the garden and the consequences of sin. He would have been familiar with the practice of sacrificing animals as an atonement for sin.

It was Lamech's son Noah, a righteous man, who built the ark and carried God's promise through the flood to new generations. The first thing Noah did after releasing the animals from the ark was to build an altar and make a sacrifice to God with the animals he had brought for that purpose. Noah and his family set about to repopulate the earth, and the record of Noah's family is found in Genesis 11. Again we find a specific genealogical list. With God's blessing Noah's family grew and multiplied. Families became clans and tribes, dividing, migrating, and slowly populating the earth. Men built cities and claimed lands as their own. Cities became nations with kings and rulers.

---

[45] 1 John 2:25.
[46] 1 John 5:11.

But why was it taking God so long to keep His promise? Some families believed and followed God; others turned away from Him and went their own way. Where was the Saviour? Had God forgotten?

No. God is all knowing, and He can't forget His promises. The reason we often struggle to understand God is because His plans and His timetable rarely coincide with ours. We're not very good at waiting, but somehow waiting and faith go hand in hand. To wait on God is to step out of time as we know it and into the presence of God. This is the place where our agenda begins to blur and where we begin to see with clarity the significance of God's eternal purpose.

A FAMILY TO CALL HIS OWN

How could He, Yahweh, Lord God Almighty, Creator and Sustainer of the universe, get through to these human creatures He loved so much? He, the King of heaven and earth, had created them to expand the pleasure and fellowship of who He is, the Great I AM, but they were so weak and frail.

He wanted men and women to love Him the way He loved them. He wanted them to be His family, but they would have to make that choice. Without choice, it wouldn't be love. He wanted to share His rulership with them, but now that Satan had worked his evil it would be difficult. Nevertheless, He would do everything possible to reach out to them and convince them of His love and His sovereignty.

If they looked at the intricacy of design and complexity in created things, they would surely see Him. Through the prophets He would give them the exact details of His plan. It would be hard for them not to recognize that such knowledge of things to come must be from Him. He would have scribes record it all: the history, the covenants, the promises. All the collected writings would be called His Word, His personal letter to humanity, straight from heaven.

His Son, Jesus Christ, was ready to take on flesh and to die to pay the debt of their sin. That provision had been in place before He created them, but He knew that skeptical humans would want proof of who Jesus was. In order to establish His Son's identity, He would need a special family on earth. He would call them and set them apart, and the world would know that they were His chosen people.

The ancient promise that had been passed down from father to son for hundreds of years was about to take on detail. That which had been hidden was ready to be unveiled, and when the time was right, God called Abram for this purpose.

Now the Lord had said to Abram: "Get out of your country, from your family and from your father's house, to a land that I will show you. I will make you a great nation; I will bless you and make your name great; and you shall be a blessing. I will bless those who bless you, and I will curse him who curses you; and in you all the families of the earth shall be blessed."[47]

This special promise is called a covenant. Unlike the covenants made between men, who voluntarily agree to their terms, God's covenant agreement with Abram was different. In this covenant God obligated Himself alone to keep the terms of the covenant. It would be done for man's benefit but without man's help or co-operation.

For when God made a promise to Abraham, because He could swear by no one greater, He swore by Himself... that by two immutable things, in which it is impossible for God to lie, we might have strong consolation.[48]

Those two immutable things were His Name and His Word. God's most holy Name is *Yahweh*. It means "the One who is self-sufficient and

---

[47] Genesis 12:1–3.
[48] Hebrews 6:13, 18.

eternally existent." By swearing on His Name God was saying that He alone had the resources to make the promise a reality and that it would last forever. By swearing on His Word God was saying that He would do it. He Himself would accomplish that which He promised. Once again we see that the promise was always about Jesus.[49]

Abram understood that there was more at stake than his own family legacy and national heritage. He understood the gospel[50] and that God's eternal purpose in this covenant was to reconcile sinful man to Himself. He must have often wondered how and when God would keep this promise, but his faith in a coming Messiah was unshakable, and he was credited with righteousness because of it. As further confirmation of the covenant, God changed Abram's name to *Abraham*, which means "father of many nations."

> When I got married I changed my surname from *Wright* to *Best*. The MC at our wedding reception was quick to point out that the "Best" man got the "Wright" girl. My sister's middle name is *Lee*. This was my grandmother's maiden surname, and it shows up regularly in each new family unit. The traditions associated with names have been passed down to us from the earliest times.
>
> Bible names often reflect the characteristics or destiny of a person or the significance of an event or place. When God called Abram to leave his home in Ur of the Chaldeans, Abram set out, not knowing where he was going but trusting God to lead the way. Because of his nomadic lifestyle Abram was called a *Hebrew*, which means "wanderer" or "one from beyond." This is how his descendants came to be called Hebrews. The words *Jew* and *Jewish* are derivatives of this. When God changed Abram's name to *Abraham*, he also changed the name of Abraham's wife from *Sarai* to *Sarah*, meaning "princess." Some Bible scholars believe that God took the *h* sounding letter from His own sacred name *Yahweh*

---

[49] Galatians 3:16.
[50] Galatians 3:8.

and added it to theirs. God in turn referred to Himself as "the God of Abraham."

The sharing of names was a sign of the covenant. It spoke of the intimate relationship between Abraham and God and was a foreshadowing of the Promised Seed, the Christ, who would be both human and divine.[51]

Years later God confirmed the covenant with Abraham's son Isaac and then again with Isaac's son Jacob. Abraham, Isaac, and Jacob, the three patriarchs, fathers of the Jewish family through whom the Messiah would be born. The ancestral line of the woman's Seed, Jesus Christ, had now been established.

A FAMILY BECOMES A NATION

Abraham's grandson Jacob also experienced a name change. On his journey home from a self-imposed exile Jacob had a personal encounter with God. As dawn was breaking the Lord said, *"Your name shall no longer be called Jacob, but Israel; for you have struggled with God and with men, and have prevailed."*[52]

Jacob's twelve sons became the twelve tribes of Israel, and God grew this family into a nation by moving them to the land of Egypt during a severe famine. These shepherd nomads were despised by the Egyptians. They were alienated and shunned in a part of Egypt called the land of Goshen. Because the family grew so quickly the Egyptians feared the Hebrew people and eventually made them slaves. Everything happened exactly as God had told Abraham.

After four hundred years of slavery in Egypt, the Hebrews emerged as a nation under the leadership of Moses. They had gone to Egypt as a family of seventy and now numbered over two million. It was time for God's chosen people, the nation of Israel, to return to Canaan, the land that God had promised to Abraham and his descendants. God had said to him, *"I am the Lord, who brought you out of Ur of the Chaldeans, to give*

---

[51] Kay Arthur, *Our Covenant God* (Colorado Springs, CO: Waterbrook Press, 1999), 171.
[52] Genesis 32:28.

you this land to inherit it"[53] and "*I give to you and your descendants after you... all the land of Canaan, as an everlasting possession.*"[54]

Early on in their journey to the Promised Land, God made a special covenant with Israel at the foot of Mount Sinai. Through their leader Moses, Israel received God's commandments and laws and promised to faithfully obey them.[55] They swore to worship and serve Yahweh alone, and in return for their faithfulness God promised that He would help them take possession of the land. He would bless his people with health, prosperity, and protection.[56]

That was their agreement. God even gave them advice on how to keep their part of the covenant. He instructed the Israelites not to intermarry with the ungodly nations that still occupied some of the land. Intermarriage with people of other faiths would not only put Israel at risk of assimilation; it would surely cause them to turn from the one true God to worship the Canaanite gods and idols. Despite countless warnings, the people repeatedly violated their agreement with God, and the words of Moses fell on deaf ears. "*The Lord will scatter you among all nations, from one end of the earth to the other.*"[57] Because of their idolatry the homeland that they had waited so long for was eventually taken from them, and rather than victory and prosperity, Israel's history became one of exile and persecution.

As a result of the broken covenant Israel suffered serious consequences, but God remained faithful. Despite their dispersion the prophet Ezekiel announced that God would provide future redemption: "*I will gather you from the peoples, assemble you from the countries where you have been scattered, and I will give you the land of Israel.*"[58] This prophecy was fulfilled on May 14, 1948, when Israel once again became a nation.

> Did you know that throughout the Jewish dispersion Israel's homeland was a dry wasteland? But God promised that in

---

[53] Genesis 15:7.
[54] Genesis 17:8.
[55] Exodus 24:7.
[56] Deuteronomy 7:12–16.
[57] Deuteronomy 28:64, NIV.
[58] Ezekiel 11:17.

a day to come *"the wilderness and the wasteland… shall rejoice and blossom as the rose."*[59]

Israel today is seen as an agricultural miracle of crops and newly planted forests. It is the only country in the world that reported a net gain of trees in the 20th century. Did you know that meteorological charts report an unexplained increase in rainfall levels as exiled Jews have returned to the land? God promised to *"give waters in the wilderness and rivers in the desert, to give drink to My people, My chosen."*[60] The population could not have survived without this.

Did you know that approximately 20 percent of Nobel prizes have been won by Jews? They have excelled in medicine, science, and technology. Jonas Salk, the creator of the polio vaccine; famous scientist Albert Einstein; and Stanley Mazor, co-creator of the microprocessor, are but a few of the most notable. Israel is His *"special treasure above all the peoples on the face of the earth,"*[61] and this persecuted race of people has brought more blessing to the earth than any other nation. Just as God promised Abraham.[62]

Today, more than ever before, the survival and presence of Israel in the world are a reminder to us of who God is and what He has done. Israel is a nation of Jewish people, but Israel is also a country, a small tract of land on the Mediterranean Sea that God gave to Abraham and his descendants. Because of Israel's tiny size and population, the rebirth of this nation in 1948 is all the more miraculous. Ironically, their survival as a race of people stems from the persecution and alienation they have suffered. The covenant they made with God at Mount Sinai was broken, but God's covenant with Abraham could not be broken. God obligated Himself to keep the Abrahamic covenant, and even though Israel was unfaithful to God, He would always be faithful to Abraham's seed.

---

[59] Isaiah 35:1.
[60] Isaiah 43:20.
[61] Deuteronomy 7:6.
[62] Genesis 12:3.

Through them, God took on flesh and established a human identity in the person of Jesus Christ, the Holy One of Israel.

The story of how God gets His family back begins with the story of Israel. It is the family heritage of we who call ourselves Christians. It is where those who believe in Jesus Christ find the roots of their faith, and… *who Jesus is changes everything!*

CHAPTER 4
Jesus, Son of Man

OUR CULTURE HAS A REAL FASCINATION WITH ANYTHING LEGAL. WHETHER IT BE BOOKS, television, or movies, a significant part of our entertainment is devoted to police stories and courtroom dramas. Whether we're reading a John Grisham novel or watching Judge Judy, there's something in us that longs to see justice served. Very often it's the evidence that determines whether or not this happens.

Lee Strobel, a former legal editor at the *Chicago Tribune*, considered himself to be an atheist. It was the evil in our world that made Strobel question God's existence, but when his wife announced that she had become a Christian he found his unbelief being challenged. He saw positive changes in her life that he couldn't explain, and he wanted to know why. That journey led him to interview the most respected scholars he could find regarding the claims of Jesus Christ.

In his book *The Case For Christ*,[63] Strobel tells the compelling story of his investigations and how he ultimately came to believe in Jesus. He looked to the Bible as his

[63] Lee Strobel, *The Case for Christ* (Grand Rapids, MI: Zondervan, 1998).

source of information because it was the record closest to the time of Jesus, but being a reporter he first had to determine whether the Bible was a trustworthy document for that purpose. His unbelieving mind set out to disprove the Bible, but after exhaustive research Strobel determined that the Bible was a credible resource. Next he tried to discredit the claims of Christ based on the teaching of the Bible, but through his investigation he came to realize the truth of who Jesus Christ is.

Unlike Strobel, when it comes to spiritual matters we quite often base our thoughts and opinions on things we've heard. Rather than searching for answers ourselves, we sometimes let our views be shaped by what others think. Usually these are people we respect, like family, friends, or teachers, but have you ever considered the possibility that they might be wrong? What if they're sincere but mistaken? Our knowledge and understanding of God should be based on what God tells us about Himself, not what others think or say. The truth about Jesus is critical because Jesus reveals the truth about God.[64]

Some people question whether Jesus was a real person in history, but doing this brings all history into question. The manuscripts that support the authenticity of the Bible far surpass the standards by which all ancient documents are judged, both in volume and timeliness. In addition to the New Testament record of His life, there were secular historians in the first century who also wrote about Jesus. There is really no basis to refute His physical presence in our world. It's who He claims to be that challenges our perspective on life. It's the words of Jesus that make people feel uncomfortable.

Jesus said that He was the promised Messiah, the fulfillment of Old Testament prophecy.[65]

He said He came to save the world.[66]

He said He would rise from the dead.[67]

---

[64] John 1:18, 12:45.
[65] Matthew 5:17; John 4:26.
[66] John 3:14–17.
[67] Matthew 20:19; Luke 18:33.

He said He was the King of the Jews.[68]

He said He was God.[69]

Masses of people loved and followed Jesus, but it was these claims that made the Jewish religious leaders angry. They hated Him and eventually had Him crucified because He confronted their hypocrisy. The reason Jesus' words evoke such an emotional response from people is that the stakes are high. Jesus not only made these claims; He went on to say that those who didn't believe in Him would die in their sin.[70] How can we be indifferent when He says that what we believe about Him is a matter of life and death?

You can deny or ignore Jesus' words, but they won't go away. Until you personally confront the person of Jesus Christ and who He is, you can never really understand the Christian faith or what it means to belong to God's family.

CALL HIM JESUS

Have you ever wondered what the name *Jesus Christ* means? In the Greek language, *Jesus* means "Saviour." The Hebrew equivalent is *Jeshua* or *Joshua*, meaning "Jehovah is salvation." The Old Testament prophets pointed to a coming *Messiah,* which means "anointed one." In the New Testament *Christos or Christ* is the Greek equivalent, also meaning the "anointed one." Jesus Christ is the anointed Saviour.

Life had been just about perfect for Joseph. He did good work as a carpenter in Nazareth and was engaged to Mary, the love of his life. The future was bright for them, but then, just two days ago, Mary told him that she was pregnant.

He was instantly consumed with feelings of anger and betrayal. Who had she been with, and what would he tell people? She said that an angel told her the child growing in her was conceived by the Holy Spirit and would be called the Son of God. Was she crazy?

He had stormed out of the house, needing to catch his

---

[68] Matthew 27:11.
[69] John 10:30.
[70] John 8:24.

breath, needing to clear his head. As he played that moment over and over in his mind, there was one thing that made him hesitate. He knew her so well. There had been a light in her eye and a calm confidence in her voice that made him wonder.

He had planned to send her away, but last night an angel had appeared to him in a dream. Or was it as dream? It was so real, and the angel's words still haunted him:

"Joseph, son of David, do not be afraid to take to you Mary your wife, for that which is conceived in her is of the Holy Spirit. And she will bring forth a Son, and you shall call His name Jesus, for He will save His people from their sins."[71]

The Old Testament prophecies concerning the birth of Christ are not shrouded in riddles or vague language. They tell us that the Messiah will come from the tribe of Judah and the house of David. The prophet Micah speaks of His birthplace, Bethlehem, and in the New Testament we find detailed accounts of the birth of Christ in the Gospel of Matthew and the Gospel of Luke. Each writer focuses on different aspects of the Christmas story, but both present Jesus as the fulfillment of Jewish prophecy.

All this was done that it might be fulfilled which was spoken by the Lord through the prophet, saying: "Behold, the virgin shall be with child, and bear a Son, and they shall call His name Immanuel," which is translated, "God with us."[72]

The prophet Isaiah also said, "*Unto us a Child is born, unto us a Son is given.*"[73] The child was born of His mother Mary, but the Son was given by God, the Father. Jesus did not have a human father. He was conceived by the Holy Spirit. He is the only begotten Son of God.

---

[71] Matthew 1:20–21.
[72] Matthew 1:22–23.
[73] Isaiah 9:6.

Matthew refers to Joseph not as Jesus' father but as *"the husband of Mary, of whom was born Jesus who is called Christ."*[74] Luke also specifies that Jesus' humanity is through His mother Mary rather than Joseph. He writes, *"Jesus… being (as was supposed) the son of Joseph, the son of Heli."*[75] People at that time assumed that Joseph was Jesus' father, but Luke is clear that Jesus' human lineage is through the line of Heli, who was Mary's father.

Jesus' connection to humanity through His mother Mary complements God's promise in the garden when God told the serpent, *"I will put enmity between you and the woman, and between your seed and her Seed."*[76] The Hebrew word for *seed* in this passage means "offspring." The ancients believed that a man sowed his "seed" in the woman's "soil" and that the role of women in procreation was passive. It wasn't until the 1800s that scientists gained a clearer understanding of human anatomy and learned that men and women are equal contributors in the creation of a new life. How incredible that the Genesis record bears witness to this truth long before men knew about the seed of women!

GENEALOGY (FROM THE GREEK *GENEA, "GENERATION"* AND *LOGOS, "KNOWLEDGE"*)

Genealogy literally means the knowledge of generations. It is the study of family and how one generation connects to another. Genealogy has established itself as a reliable evidentiary science and is often called on to provide valuable or missing information about family relationships. It's enabled many adoptees to locate and reunite with their birth families. It's been useful in determining the incidence and probability of disease where there is a family history of hereditary medical conditions.

Even today bloodline relationships continue to be a determining factor in the distribution of an inheritance. Knowledge of family relationships is key to understanding how the assets of an estate should be passed on. We experienced this first-hand a few years ago.

---

[74] Matthew 1:16.

[75] Luke 3:23.

[76] Genesis 3:15.

> After his mother passed away, my husband, Jim, received a phone call about a cousin of hers who died in 1983 without a will. Cousin Bessie was unknown to us. She had been a widow with no children and had spent her latter years in a psychiatric hospital. Because nothing was known about her family at the time of her death, the public guardian and trustee (PGT) took control of her $7,000 estate.
>
> After many years the PGT sought the help of the genealogical society to see if Bessie had any living relatives. Genealogists at the society were able to identify Bessie's parents and five siblings, but none of them were still living. Eventually they identified who the children of Bessie's siblings were, and these eight cousins made up the beneficiary group.
>
> The estate, which had grown to $42,000 over thirty years, was divided into eight portions. The problem was that seven of the eight cousins, including my mother-in-law, were also deceased. Before the estate could be distributed, the surviving beneficiaries of the deceased cousins had to be located. In the end there were thirty people who shared in the estate, and we learned first-hand the important role that genealogists play in our complex world.

We should not be surprised to find genealogical records in the Bible. The early history of the human family is wrapped up in the carefully preserved records of "who begat who" in Genesis chapter 5. The meticulous detail of this data provides strong evidence of the Bible's historical accuracy, and the genealogies that we find in 1 Chronicles 1–9 form the backbone of Jewish history.

Even in ancient times genealogies were a necessary determinant of "rights" with respect to family ownership and rulership because one's rights were determined by one's birth. The recorded kinship of rulers and nobles established the legitimacy of claims involving both wealth and power. Old Testament genealogies were carefully guarded through centuries of national upheaval, and they revealed the Jewish family line through whom the Messiah would come. This promise to the world was transmitted over a period of four thousand years, a fact unparalleled in history. Both Luke and Matthew use these records with confidence to cast different perspectives on the human identity of Jesus Christ.

BEHOLD THE MAN

After a detailed account of the events surrounding the birth of Christ, Luke uses the Old Testament records to demonstrate Jesus' bloodline. He traces Jesus' human ancestry back to David using the family line of Mary, Jesus' mother. From David he then continues to trace the ancestral line back to the beginning of humanity, showing Jesus to be a descendant of Adam, the first created man. This single line of origin to Adam not only confirms Jesus' human descent; it also confirms the Genesis record of man's origin.[77]

The connection between Adam and Jesus is extremely important because it has to do with man's lost authority over God's creation. Authority is the right to rule, and in his book *Authority in Prayer*, Dutch Sheets explains that God as the author of creation has full rights to what He created. "The root concept behind authority is authorship, not as in writing but as in origination or creation. One has authority over what one authors."[78] When God delegated His authority over earth to Adam He willingly forfeited His right to intervene in the choices that Adam would make. Through deception and disobedience Adam gave his God-given authority over earth to Satan. The apostle John would later write that "*the whole world is in the power of the evil one.*"[79]

Jesus Himself referred to Satan as "*the ruler of this world.*"[80] At the beginning of His ministry when tempted by Satan in the wilderness, Jesus didn't dispute the devil's claim of authority over the world:

> *The devil led him [Jesus] up to a high place and showed him in an instant all the kingdoms of the world. And he said to him, "I will give you all their authority and splendor; it has been given to me,*

---

[77] Luke 3:38.
[78] Dutch Sheets, *Authority in Prayer* (Minneapolis, MN: Bethany House, 2006), 23.
[79] 1 John 5:19, RSV.
[80] John 12:31.

and I can give it to anyone I want to. If you worship me, it will all be yours.[81]

The sin of Adam, God's perfect human creation, gave entrance to sin and death.[82] Only the death of another perfect man would be able to pay this debt of sin, and Jesus was that perfect man. Because He was conceived by the Holy Spirit of God, Jesus was not born in sin like the rest of us. If Jesus had not been a perfect human being, then His death on the cross would have been useless. He would have simply died for His own sin, and He would have stayed in the tomb.

Jesus' resurrection from the dead proves that the penalty for our sin was paid in full.[83] Having paid the debt, Jesus received back man's right of rulership that had been lost in the garden. As He left earth Jesus said, *"All authority has been given to Me in heaven and on earth."*[84] He delivered mankind from sin and death and in Himself restored man's authority over creation. This was only possible because He was fully human.

BEHOLD YOUR KING

Matthew also uses the Jewish genealogical records to substantiate the claims of Jesus, specifically the legitimacy of kingly rights associated with His birth and heritage. According to the prophets, the Messiah would be a descendant of Abraham[85] and an heir to King David's throne.[86]

Royal succession to the throne of Israel was through the father's line, so in a descending order of "who begat who" from Abraham to David and then from David to Jesus, Matthew uses Joseph's ancestral line to show that Jesus meets these requirements and is a rightful heir. Joseph did not "beget" Jesus, but as Joseph's adopted son under Roman law, Jesus would have greater legal rights than a natural-born son. Jesus claimed to be the King of the Jews because through Joseph's line it was His right to do so.

---

[81] Luke 4:5–7, NIV.
[82] Romans 5:12.
[83] Romans 4:25.
[84] Matthew 28:18.
[85] Genesis 3:16.
[86] 1 Chronicles 17:14.

It was over thirty years now since Jesus had ministered on earth, and yet the events of those days were indelibly etched in Matthew's mind. He had been a Jewish tax collector when Jesus called him to be a disciple. Little did he know in those early days that he would witness the murder of his Master and Lord at the hand of his own people.

Jesus was their Messiah and their King, but the Jews had rejected Him and demanded His crucifixion. Matthew remembered Jesus' heart wrenching cry of love and pain just days before His death: "*O Jerusalem, Jerusalem, the one who kills the prophets and stones those who are sent to her! How often I wanted to gather your children together, as a hen gathers her chicks under her wings, but you were not willing!*"[87]

The people wanted deliverance from the oppression of Rome. They wanted a leader who would fulfill God's promise to Abraham. *"To your descendants I will give this land."*[88] They wanted an earthly king who would restore them to their homeland. Often when he prayed now the Spirit of God brought vivid images and words to Matthew's mind. He felt a growing compulsion to write and explain the truth about Jesus to his people.

From beginning to end the gospel of Matthew presents Jesus as Israel's Messiah and rightful King. Matthew is writing to share this good news with his fellow Jews. I'm sure he had no idea that his words would one day find a worldwide audience.

The Jews longed for an earthly king, but God reveals through Matthew that the kingdom of the Messiah encompasses both heaven and earth. Matthew writes about the teachings of Jesus with a specific focus on the Kingdom of God, pointing to a day when Jesus Christ will come back again to earth. The anointed Saviour of mankind will return in the company of His holy angels to rule His kingdom with all the

---

[87] Matthew 23:37.
[88] Genesis 12:7.

power and authority of God. He reigns as the rightful King because He is fully human. But let's not forget... *He rules with power and authority because He is fully God.*

CHAPTER 5
Jesus, Son of God

JEWISH HISTORY, PROPHECIES AND GENEALOGIES COME TOGETHER LIKE THE CONNECTING dots of a puzzle. Dot by dot a picture of the person of Jesus Christ emerges. The Gospels add colour and depth to the portrait, filling in the background and illuminating the reality of His physical presence on earth two thousand years ago.

I feel fortunate to have grown up during a time when there was Bible reading and prayer in schools. I thought everybody knew who Jesus was, but when I attended the Alpha program a few years ago, I began to realize that this wasn't always the case.

Alpha is a popular program that provides a casual environment where people can ask questions about life and the Christian faith. I remember listening with interest as people shared their thoughts on the question "Who is Jesus?" Sarah, a young teenage girl, said she'd been taught that Jesus was a good man and teacher who lived two thousand years ago. Ben, an older man who had gone to church all his life, said that he understood Jesus was human but couldn't see how Jesus could also be God. People were open and honest in

> their sharing, but the opportunity to respond was limited because Alpha is meant to be a journey of self-discovery.
>
> I felt frustrated as I drove home that night, and the question still hung in the air. "Who is Jesus?" How do I respond to a teenage girl who doesn't own a Bible and thinks Jesus is a good teacher? How do I explain truth to a man who's gone to church all his life and yet doesn't have any assurance that Jesus is God?

Jesus wasn't just a guy who showed up on the streets of Jerusalem claiming to be God. Jesus was a Jew from an established family clan, from the tribe of Judah with connections to the Jewish priesthood.[89] His lineage and ancestry were well documented. He met every qualification and fulfilled every prophecy regarding the promised Messiah.[90] He grew up as a carpenter's son but from a young age displayed a wisdom beyond His years. He didn't sit under the teaching of local scribes and rabbis, but when He was only twelve Joseph and Mary found Him in the temple with the teachers, and *"all who heard Him were astonished at His understanding and answers."*[91]

I thought again about Lee Strobel's experience. His search for truth had taken Him to the Bible. Even though he approached it with skepticism at first, Strobel found it to be authentic. This is important because the Bible not only tells us about Jesus' life; it tells us what Jesus had to say about Himself. If I want to explain who Jesus is to people like Ben and Sarah, then the Bible is the best place to look for answers.

JESUS SAID HE WAS GOD

Each of the Gospels—Matthew, Mark, Luke, and John—has a unique perspective on the person of Jesus Christ, but at the same time there is incredible consistency across these records. All four tell us that wherever Jesus went, masses of people followed. He healed the sick, performed miracles, and announced that the Kingdom of God was at hand. He

---

[89] Luke 1:5, 36–40.
[90] Isaiah 7:14, 9:6; Psalm 132:11; Micah 5:2; Genesis 49:10.
[91] Luke 2:47.

spoke hope and deliverance into a world that was all too familiar with violence and idolatry.

But Jesus could say or do little without the religious hierarchy becoming furious. They were outraged that He would refer to God as His Father. On one occasion when Jesus said, *"I and My Father are one,"*[92] they took up stones to stone Him, but Jesus stood His ground. *"Many good works I have shown you from My Father. For which of those works do you stone Me?"*[93] Their opinion and their opposition were clear. *"For a good work we do not stone You, but for blasphemy, and because You, being a man, make Yourself God."*[94] No uncertainty there. The reason the Pharisees wanted to kill Jesus was because He claimed to be God.

Hundreds of years earlier when God chose Moses to lead the Israelites out of Egypt, Moses asked God what to say when the Israelites wanted to know the name of God. God responded to Moses by saying, *"I AM WHO I AM... Thus you shall say to the children of Israel, 'I AM has sent me to you.'"*[95] One day as Jesus was engaged in an intense discussion with the Pharisees He repeatedly used that name, "I AM," in reference to Himself.[96] The debate escalated, and finally, in His most stunning confrontation, Jesus declared, *"Before Abraham was, I AM."*[97] Jesus applied the very name of God to Himself, God's most holy name, Yahweh, the One who is totally self-sufficient and eternally existent. He claimed to be God, and rightfully so. His claim rested on hundreds of years of Jewish history, a history that went all the way back to Adam. Everything the Pharisees needed to know about Him was in the Scriptures, but their religious thinking blinded them to the truth.

It had been another long and frustrating day, but how He loved to minister to the people! Just a few hours earlier He had saved a woman from stoning by pointing His finger back at the sins of her accusers. That was always His greatest

---

[92] John 10:30.
[93] John 10:32.
[94] John 10:33.
[95] Exodus 3:14.
[96] John 8:24, 28.
[97] John 8:58.

challenge. How could He, Jesus, the Son of God, get through to the religious leaders of His people Israel?

Hypocrites they were, those Pharisees, always testing and provoking Him. They could see divine power at work in His miracles, but they held tight to their rituals and traditions. He was their Messiah, the anointed Saviour, but they believed that only their self-righteous good works could save them.

He spoke in parables, explaining Himself in so many different ways. They knew the temple was God's presence in their midst, and He used its symbolism to show them that He was now that presence. He was the light of the world, the bread of life, and the living water. He was the fulfillment of the promise made to Adam and Eve in the garden, but His words fell on deaf ears. The Pharisees didn't want to believe. They wanted Him dead.

The priests and leaders knew the Messiah was to come from the line of David and be born in Bethlehem,[98] but they only saw Jesus of Nazareth, the son of Mary and Joseph. Jesus challenged their thinking, and tempers often flared. "*You both know Me, and you know where I am from; and I have not come of Myself, but He who sent Me is true, whom you do not know. But I know Him, for I am from Him, and He sent Me.*"[99]

It was in the midst of heated debates in the temple with Israel's most learned that Jesus claimed to be God. They should have known who He was. Perhaps deep down inside they did know. Maybe they just didn't want Him rocking their religious boat.

It's not a whole lot different today. How do you react to what Jesus says? There really aren't a lot of options. He was either speaking the truth about Himself or He was a liar. C. S. Lewis, a great Cambridge professor and theologian, was also very skeptical in his younger years, but after searching for truth in the Bible he came to believe in Jesus. Here's what he says:

---

[98] John 7:42.
[99] John 7:28–29.

I am trying here to prevent anyone saying the really foolish thing that people often say about Him: "I'm ready to accept Jesus as a great moral teacher, but I don't accept His claim to be God." That is the one thing we must not say. A man who was merely a man and said the sort of things Jesus said would not be a great moral teacher. He would either be a lunatic…or else he would be the Devil of Hell. You must make your choice. Either this man was, and is, the Son of God: or else a madman or something worse. You can shut Him up for a fool, you can spit at Him and kill Him as a demon; or you can fall at His feet and call Him Lord and God. But let us not come with any patronizing nonsense about His being a great human teacher. He has not left that open to us. He did not intend to.[100]

THE WITNESS OF THE WORD

The debates, the accusations, and the arguments always came back to His words, to the things Jesus said. His words were as powerful as the miracles He performed. The crowds found hope in the wisdom of His words. He calmed the winds and waves with the word of authority. With words of life He called forth Lazarus from the grave.

But the words that brought healing to some roused anger in others. Once when the Pharisees sent officers to arrest Jesus they came back empty-handed. They said they couldn't arrest Jesus because "*No man ever spoke like this Man!*"[101]

Jesus knew that the Jewish legal system required two or three witnesses to substantiate a claim or testify in a dispute.[102] One day He said to His opponents, "*If I bear witness of Myself, My witness is not true.*"[103] He recognized that the claims He made regarding His identity were incomplete unless they were backed by witnesses. He didn't expect the religious leaders to accept His word alone. He wanted them to listen to what the witnesses had to say before they cast judgment, and the first witness He called on was John the Baptist. John was the one

---

[100] C. S. Lewis, *Mere Christianity* (New York, NY: Macmillan-Collier, 1960), 55–56.
[101] John 7:46.
[102] Deuteronomy 19:15.
[103] John 5:31.

who heralded His coming and baptized Him. It was John who publicly declared, *"I have seen and testified that this is the Son of God."*[104] Then there was His disciple Peter, who said, *"You are the Christ, the Son of the living God."*[105]

After His death and resurrection Jesus was seen several times by His disciples[106] and on one occasion by a gathering of over five hundred people.[107] It seems reasonable that God would want the truth about His Son to be confirmed by many witnesses. The Bible uses eyewitness testimony to validate that Jesus is who He claims to be, but Jesus then points to another witness. *"But I have a greater witness than John's; for the works which the Father has given Me to finish—the very works that I do—bear witness of Me, that the Father has sent Me."*[108]

Jesus' challenge to us today is the same as it was to the Pharisees hundreds of years ago. He wants us to hear what the Word of God tells us about Him, and He wants us to watch and see Him at work in our lives.

> Jim and I enjoy boating, and one year decided to take a trip through the Trent Severn Waterway. The first day went well, but on the second day, right when we were in the middle of Buckhorn Lake, I suddenly smelled smoke. I yelled, and Jim quickly turned off the engine. As he lifted the engine cover thick black smoke came billowing out.
>
> Thankfully we didn't have a fire, but what do you do when you're stuck in the middle of a lake? We had a small dinghy with us, and Jim thought perhaps he could tow us to shore. I thought, *That little dinghy isn't going to tow this big boat.* He gave it a try, but the boat was just too heavy.
>
> Then it occurred to me—this might be a good time to pray. I went below deck and got right to the point,. "Lord, having a boat and taking this trip were choices we made. Our

---

[104] John 1:34.

[105] Matthew 16:16.

[106] 1 Corinthians 15:5.

[107] 1 Corinthians 15:6.

[108] John 5:36.

choices have consequences, and we take responsibility for them. I'm not asking You to miraculously fix our engine. Lord, I just need to know that You're here with us and that You'll help us get through this." I went back up on deck, and there was Jim, out in the little dinghy, tracking straight toward a marina on shore with our big boat in tow.

Later that evening when all the excitement died down I asked him, "You weren't going anywhere with the dinghy, and then it suddenly started to work. What happened?"

Jim looked at me with a smile. "Jeanne, the wind shifted and pushed us forward. As we were both praying, the wind shifted."

He makes winds his messengers.[109]

THE WORD BECAME FLESH

We've all felt the encouragement of being told we look nice or that we've done a good job. Likewise, we've felt the sting of angry words spoken thoughtlessly and in haste. Words are powerful because words are more than just words. Words influence how we think and direct the things we do.

Dabar is Hebrew for "word."[110] It signifies a word spoken as well as the activities associated with that word. Because of their knowledge of God, the Jews understood that there was an association between words and actions. From early on in their history they knew that the God who had committed His written word to their keeping was the same God who spoke the world into existence and created everything in it.

> *By the word of the Lord the heavens were made, And all the host of them by the breath of His mouth… For He spoke, and it was done; He commanded, and it stood fast.*[111]

---

[109] Psalm 104:4, NIV.

[110] James Strong, "Hebrew-Aramaic Dictionary" in *The Strongest Strong's Exhaustive Concordance* (Grand Rapids, MI: Zondervan, 2001), s.v. "dabar."

[111] Psalm 33:6–9.

For many years the apostles faithfully preached the gospel, and many people believed in Jesus, but now everything had changed. Titus had besieged Jerusalem (AD 70), and over 600,000 Jews lost their lives in the slaughter. The apostle John felt God directing him to leave the holy city and go to Ephesus. As he reflected back on his days with Jesus, John vividly remembered the day Jesus had called him to leave his father's fishing business to be a "fisher of men."

He had known Jesus all his life. His mother, Salome, and Jesus' mother, Mary, were sisters,[112] and after Jesus' death and resurrection he had stayed in Jerusalem to care for them. John was an eyewitness to everything that had been said and done, and the Hebrew manuscripts in which he had recorded it were his most treasured possession.

After arriving in Ephesus, John began translating his manuscripts into the Greek language. He recalled that the Greek Gentiles believed in the "logos." They saw order, reason, and logic in the created things around them. To the Greeks, the logos was the wisdom that steered the universe and manifested itself in man's speech and activity. John used this familiar word to help the Gentiles understand that Jesus was God:

In the beginning was the Word [the logos], and the Word was with God, and the Word [the logos] was God. He was in the beginning with God... And the Word [the logos] became flesh and dwelt among us.[113]

Jesus was with the Father in the beginning before anything was created. "*For there are three that bear witness in heaven: the Father, the*

---

[112] Mark 16:1; Matthew 27:56; John 19:25. Note: editors of *The New Bible Dictionary* suggest that in the three Scriptures noted, Zebedee's wife, Salome, and Mary's sister are one and the same person. See J. D. Douglas et al., eds., *The New Bible Dictionary* (Grand Rapids, MI: Wm. B. Eerdmans Publishing Co., 1965), 1125.

[113] John 1:1–2, 14.

Word, and the Holy Spirit; and these three are one."[114] To say that God's Word goes out to do something is the same as to say Jesus has gone out to do something. "*All things were made through Him, and without Him nothing was made that was made.*"[115] "*By faith we understand that the worlds were framed by the word of God.*"[116]

> *For in him all things were created, in heaven and on earth, visible and invisible, whether thrones or dominions or principalities or authorities—all things were created through him and for him. He is before all things, and in him all things hold together.*[117]

Did you get that last part? In Him everything holds together. He is the power of God that holds every atom in place, and without the power of the Word holding the created things together, nothing would exist. John declared that Jesus is the Word of God, that Jesus is God.

What's your verdict? How do you respond to Jesus? You can take up stones like the Pharisees and try to kill Him with words of ridicule and unbelief, but the record of His Word stands. You can belittle Him by speaking His name carelessly or in anger, but He has forgiven you. You can even try to ignore Him, but the testimony of the witnesses and the evidence of creation are overwhelming. "*His invisible attributes are clearly seen, being understood by the things that are made, even His eternal power and Godhead, so that they are without excuse.*"[118] You can respond to Jesus in whatever way you choose, or, as C. S. Lewis said, "You can fall at His feet and call Him Lord and God."[119]

God lets you choose because without choice there is no love.

---

[114] 1 John 5:7.
[115] John 1:3.
[116] Hebrews 11:3.
[117] Colossians 1:16–17, RSV.
[118] Romans 1:20.
[119] Lewis, *Mere Christianity*, 55–56.

CHAPTER 6
God's Good News

THERE ARE A MULTITUDE OF RELIGIONS IN THE WORLD TODAY, EACH CLAIMING TO HAVE A corner on truth. How can we possibly find truth in the midst of all this conflict and contradiction?

Many people now claim that there is no truth, that truth is only relative to a given situation. They say that truth can't be absolute. But guess what? Saying that truth isn't absolute is an absolute statement! Let's not make life any more complicated than it already is. Of course there's truth.

Jesus said He was truth and that the reason He came into the world was to testify to the truth.[120] People love to philosophize about truth and dance around religion because they trust in their own wisdom. Something inside of us wants to believe that we have a part to play in finding God and that our effort counts for something, but the truth is, it's just the opposite.

> Humanity faced an insoluble dilemma: no matter how hard we tried, we could never find an infinite God by using finite human resources called religion. Fortunately for us, God

---

[120] John 18:37.

solved the problem Himself, because He is the only one who could. Mankind's problem did not take God by surprise. In His omniscience—His all-knowing nature—God knew before time began that we would never find Him without His help. Therefore, God launched a journey. He set out to find *us*. God is the chaser and we are the pursued.[121]

After Adam and Eve sinned they went into hiding. They didn't go looking for God. It was God who came looking for them. Religion is man's attempt to restore his relationship with God. Religion is man's substitute for what he lost in the garden, but salvation will never be found in the rules or traditions or doctrines of men.

Every religion in the world is about finite man doing his best to reach up and lay hold of infinite God. This is where Christianity differs from religion. It's all about Jesus and how He alone meets our deepest need. Jesus said the truth would make us free.[122] This is God's good news!

ANOTHER GOSPEL

One Sunday in July a few years ago, my husband and I decided to visit a church in a nearby town. The people were warm and welcoming, but I was a little puzzled as the worship team stepped forward and began leading us in singing Sarah McLachlan's song "Ice Cream." "Your love is better than ice cream. Better than anything else that I've tried."

I learned later on that we were at what's called a seeker-friendly church. The thinking behind this approach is that churches can dramatically increase attendance by giving the unchurched multitudes what they want—an upbeat gospel with a feel-good message. Unfortunately, neither ice cream nor church attendance have much to do with our salvation.

---

[121] Myles Munroe, "Discovering the Origin and Purpose of Man, " chapter 1 in *Rediscovering the Kingdom* (Shippensburg, PA: Destiny Image Publishers, 2010), p. 22.
[122] John 8:32.

The Bible warns us not to add to its message or take away from it,[123] but we've been doing this from the beginning of time. Before Adam and Eve disobeyed God, they changed His Word. God told Adam not to eat fruit from the tree of the knowledge of good and evil. It's not clear whether Adam misquoted God to Eve or Eve misquoted God apart from Adam, but she did add to the message by saying they were not to eat *or touch* the tree.[124]

The love of embellishing the truth appears to be in our genes, but here's the point. They failed to take God's Word seriously. He told them if they ate the fruit they would die, but then the serpent came along and twisted the message. He said to Eve, "*You will not surely die… you will be like God, knowing good and evil.*"[125] Rather than turning to God to clarify this contradiction Eve looked to her own wisdom. She wanted to be like God, and so she allowed herself to be deceived by a half-truth.

If death wasn't the outcome of our rebellion against God, then we wouldn't need to care so much about whether we're saved or lost. But death was the consequence of Adam and Eve's sin, and death is the consequence of my sin and yours.[126] Death is inevitable, and death is final.

God's good news is that there is salvation from sin and death through belief in the death and resurrection of Jesus Christ. In Jesus there is new life and hope. The gospel is that simple, and anything else is *another gospel*. God actually gets pretty ticked off when people change His Word. "*If anyone preaches any other gospel to you than what you have received, let him be accursed.*"[127]

Unfortunately, when we misunderstand or question God's Word, it's not unusual for us to change it to suit ourselves. The garden experience is recorded for our benefit so that we might learn from Adam and Eve's mistakes, but thousands of years later history continues to repeat itself. We're still changing the Word of God by emphasizing some parts and leaving others out. Talking about the love of God and comparing it to

---

[123] Revelation 22:18–19.
[124] Genesis 3:3.
[125] Genesis 3:4–5.
[126] Romans 6:23.
[127] Galatians 1:9.

ice cream makes us feel good. Talking about the blood of Christ—not so much. But one without the other is only half the truth.

THE DAY THAT JESUS DIED

The heart of the gospel is the cross of Jesus Christ. It's the focal point of all history because that's where all the sins of humanity—all the evil, all the ugliness, all the brutality—were laid on Jesus. *"He made Him who knew no sin to be sin for us, that we might become the righteousness of God in Him."*[128]

I can't even begin to imagine what it was like the day that Jesus died. It was during the celebration of the Jewish Passover, and the narrow, dusty roads leading to Jerusalem were packed with pilgrims. Outside the city at Calvary, the stench of humanity filled the air under the hot sun. Mob mentality brought the cruelty of men's hearts to life as they waited expectantly for blood to be shed. Roman soldiers, hardened by the daily routine of crucifixion, nailed hands and feet to crosses with no more emotion than the lifeless gods they worshipped. And all the while, a mother watched.

Arm in arm, Mary and Salome pressed through the crowd. Finally, there was a break, and Mary caught a glimpse of her Son. His beautiful face was swollen and bruised. The flesh on His back was ripped and raw. She watched as they nailed Him to the cross, and her knees buckled under the horror of it all.

As Salome and her son, John, lifted Mary to her feet, Mary's memory drifted back to the day she and Joseph had brought the baby Jesus to the temple. The prophet Simeon had told her that a sword would pierce her spirit, and today the pain of fulfilled prophecy seared her soul. Standing near the cross, Mary looked up and remembered Jesus' words: *"And I, if I am lifted up from the earth, will draw all peoples to Myself."*[129] His battered face was

---

[128] 2 Corinthians 5:21.
[129] John 12:32.

expressionless, but He caught her eye, and his gaze spoke love to her heart. With cracked, dry lips and gasping voice he said, "*Woman, behold your son!*"[130] To John He said, "*Behold your mother!*"[131] The sky turned black. A Roman soldier thrust a spear into Jesus' side. Her son was dead, and Mary wept.

The heart of God's good news is the cross, and yet there's something in us that is repulsed by it. The crucifixion of Jesus was the cruellest and most unjust murder the world has ever witnessed. It offends our sensibilities, and we're not prepared for the emotions that it stirs in us.

The sight of blood from a cut or wound can be overwhelming to some. Can you imagine the bloody mess that day on Calvary? Even those who say they believe try to lessen the horror of the cross by "sanitizing" what happened that day. Many paintings of the crucifixion show little blood. They cover the Saviour's nakedness with a loin cloth and almost never picture a beaten and battered body. Crosses of gold and silver hang in stark contrast to the blood-soaked timber. I can never understand the extent of what God accomplished at Calvary until I realize that Jesus literally hung in my place that day and that the punishment did indeed match the crime.

Humanity's debt was fully paid the day that Jesus died. His death was once for all, and God's wrath against sin and evil was satisfied at the cross. There is no further sacrifice to be made. The power of God met the power of evil head-on at the cross, and God prevailed. The Father who wants His children to come home pursues us and says, "I love you so much that I sent My Only Son to die in your place." "*There is no other name under heaven given among men by which we must be saved.*"[132] He is the way, the truth, and the life.[133] The only way to connect with the Father is through His Son.

---

[130] John 19:26.
[131] John 19:27.
[132] Acts 4:12.
[133] John 14:6.

WHAT ARE WE MISSING?

> I'm blessed to have a husband who is "handy." He loves building and fixing things, and although some women envy me, there are moments when the next project strikes fear in my heart. It's those two simple words "assembly required" that ushers in a feeling of dread. Diagrams are a maze of arrows pointing every which way, and instructions are impossible to decipher. Whether it's a bookcase or a barbecue, you know that some part will go missing, and until it's found things just won't come together. It won't make sense. It won't work.
>
> The last few years I've spent a lot of time pondering why people who profess to believe in Jesus often lack the love, joy, and peace that the Father promises His children. Why do so many Christians live contrary to the "house rules" that God teaches His family? Why is it sometimes difficult to reconcile our faith with the reality of life? The conclusion I've reached is this: Something is missing in our understanding of the gospel.

Salvation from sin and death is possible by believing in Jesus Christ, but before I can see my need of a Saviour, I have to understand what sin is. Sin is failing to acknowledge that God as my Creator has the right to tell me what's right and what's wrong. When I reject the King's law, I reject Him. Like Eve, the motive behind my sin is a desire to play God. I want to be in control of my life, and every time God says "Thou shalt not" it reminds me that I'm not God. In his book *A Tale of Two Sons*, John MacArthur describes sin this way: "When we sin, we show disdain for God's fatherly love as well as His holy authority. To sin is to deny God His place. It is an expression of hatred against God. It is tantamount to wishing He were dead."[134]

---

[134] John MacArthur, *A Tale of Two Sons* (Nashville, TN: Thomas Nelson, 2008).

The Bible often describes sin in terms of the things we do and how we treat other people,[135] but it also describes sin as a powerful force that attacks and controls us and refuses to let go.[136] I can be deceived by sin, and it can hinder my ability to respond to God's call to come home. Sin is not just that long laundry list of bad behaviours that I criticize in others and then repeatedly practice myself. These acts of sin are evidence of a sinful heart, but at the centre of a sinful heart is pride in myself and rebellion against my Creator, my King.

> *Pride* is turning away from God specifically to take satisfaction in self… *Covetousness* is turning away from God to find satisfaction in things… *Lust* is turning away from God to find satisfaction in sex… *Bitterness* is turning away from God to find satisfaction in revenge… *Impatience* is turning away from God to find satisfaction in your own uninterrupted plans of action… But deeper than all these forms of unbelief is the unbelief of pride, because self-determination and self-exaltation lie behind all these other sinful dispositions. Every turning from God— for anything—presumes a kind of autonomy or independence that is the essence of pride.[137]

God says, "*There is none righteous… none who seeks after God… none who does good.*"[138] No matter how "good" or "bad" I perceive myself or others to be, no one is able to live up to God's standard of perfection. We're all broken, and we can't fix ourselves.

It's not how many sins I commit that makes me guilty. It's not how bad my sin is that condemns me. It's simply the fact of my sin. I'm born with Adam's genes, a sinner in God's court, where my sin establishes my guilt and condemns me to death. We're all lost, and there are no degrees of lostness. The part we're missing is that we can't save ourselves. Nothing I do can remove the sentence of death that lies over me—no church

---

[135] Romans 1:29–32.
[136] Genesis 4:7.
[137] John Piper, *Battling Unbelief* (Colorado Springs, CO: Multnomah Books, 2007), 40.
[138] Romans 3:10–12; see also Isaiah 64:6.

attendance, no amount of money, no good deed, no self-improvement. I need to be rescued. I need a Saviour. I cannot save myself.

It's easy for people like myself who were taught to "be good" and "do good" to believe that God has a holy scorecard and that a high score on the goodness scale is my ticket to heaven. Somehow it's more reassuring to believe that I can earn salvation and that God owes me, but this is the deceptive thinking of religion. This is man's way of reaching God, and this kind of thinking is *another gospel*.

Religion always wants you to believe that your salvation is the result of what you do. Believing that salvation requires faith in the grace and mercy of God alone makes me feel vulnerable. It's especially difficult for religious people to acknowledge their hopelessness and helplessness, but God says this: "*For by grace you have been saved through faith, and that not of yourselves; it is the gift of God, not of works, lest anyone should boast.*"[139] Let's not change and embellish the truth like Eve.

> I remember seeing the movie *The Passion of the Christ* for the first time. I went to the theatre alone to view the film objectively. Many people were weeping, but I braced myself against the emotion of it. I came away thinking it was a good historical representation but that the brutality against Christ had been overdone. How could Jesus endure having the flesh ripped off His back and still be on His feet?
>
> Two years later as Easter approached I went to see the movie again. In the interim God had been teaching me about my sin and rebellion and guilt. He had opened my eyes to my helplessness and hopelessness. This time I viewed the film as if I were a participant, knowing that it was my sin that Jesus bore. As I watched the soldiers nail Jesus to the cross I realized that no human being could endure this kind of agony. Only God's Son could bear the punishment that should have been mine. Jesus died so that I might live.

---

[139] Ephesians 2:8–9.

My heart was broken, and tears of repentance flowed
that day. Because of His love for me, God sent His Son to die
in my place.

The gospel opens your eyes to the truth of who you are and all that the Father has done for you in Jesus Christ. The gospel of Jesus Christ is your road map home. If the demands of religion have left you exhausted and disheartened, Jesus is the door to new life. If you're lost and in a dark place, He's the light at the end of the tunnel. If you don't know which way to turn, He's your guide. Jesus is the way, the truth and the life.

Come home with empty hands and an open heart, and receive the forgiveness for which He died. Let His love wash over you and make you clean. There is salvation from sin and death when you believe in Jesus. This is the gospel, and…*this is God's good news!*

CHAPTER 7
Faith and Fathers

DOUBT COMES NATURALLY TO HUMAN BEINGS. IT'S MY NATURE TO DOUBT AND QUESTION things because as a human being I don't have all the answers. The universe is full of mysteries that I will never be able to explain. I have doubts about people too, because I know the human heart isn't always kind and loving. *What does she want? Where is he coming from?*

And then, of course, there are times when we all question God. In a way that's a good thing. It shows that we believe He's personal, a God to whom we can talk. Doubt about God isn't reserved for unbelievers. Believers are troubled by doubts and questions as well, and we find evidence of this where we would least expect it.

Jesus' disciples travelled and ministered with Him for three years, and yet following His death and resurrection, these men, who called themselves His friends, had serious doubts. Thomas in particular had a tough time.

> *Now Thomas, called the Twin, one of the twelve, was not with them when Jesus came. The other disciples therefore said to him, "We have seen the Lord." So he said to them, "Unless I see in His hands the print of the nails, and put my finger into the print of the nails, and put my hand into His side, I will not believe." And*

after eight days His disciples were again inside, and Thomas with them. Jesus came, the doors being shut, and stood in the midst, and said, "Peace to you!" Then He said to Thomas, "Reach your finger here, and look at My hands; and reach your hand here, and put it into My side. Do not be unbelieving, but believing." And Thomas answered and said to Him, "My Lord and my God!"[140]

The disciples demanded proof of His resurrection. They were men who needed answers. They didn't listen to rumours or take anything for granted. They had to see for themselves, and what they found changed them. The shock of Calvary had left them reeling, but the presence of the living Lord in their midst relieved all doubt.

Jesus knew exactly what Thomas needed and confronted him personally. The proof for Thomas was found in Jesus. This was when his doubt gave way to belief.

The disciples went on to preach the gospel and establish the Christian church. They were martyred for what they believed in and for what they knew to be true because a life that encounters the living Son of God is forever changed.

BILL'S STORY

Bill had been married for fourteen years and had two kids. After building and selling houses for several years, a downturn in the economy left him wondering what to do next. Being an entrepreneur, he decided to start a frozen food business, but its future was unknown at that point.

Around the same time, his wife, Audrey, told him she had become a Christian, and this only added to his stress. Audrey was a teacher, and after her friends at the teachers' Christian fellowship told her about Jesus, she became a believer. Bill knew these people and enjoyed socializing with them, but when it came to spiritual things he thought they were "religious nuts."

---

[140] John 20:24–28.

Bill had never read the Bible and sometimes found himself cornered in their discussions. He wanted to tear apart their "fable founded faith," but to do that he would have to read the Bible. And so he began reading, not to confirm what they were telling him but to back his own argument against them. He would sit in the evening with a glass of liquor in one hand and the Bible in the other.

Here is Bill's own description of those days: "I began to search the Scriptures, and although I was not searching for the right reasons I was certainly searching in the right place. My business was uncertain, I was drinking heavily, and my life and marriage were shaky. My insatiable desire for wealth, power, and prestige had been dealt a blow, and I was struggling with feelings of humiliation and defeat. I hated my life and blamed others. I felt alone in the world."

Conviction was growing in Bill's heart as Audrey and her friends prayed for him. He had always believed that the Bible was just a collection of stories and myths because that's what he had been taught, but as he searched for some statement or error that would back his argument, something was happening. The words of Jesus were beginning to make a powerful impression on him.

Bill knew he had reached a crossroad in his life. "It became apparent to me that there was a kind of activity and life and friendship in this world of which I had no prior knowledge. Something was happening, and I didn't know what it was, but my belligerence was giving way to bewilderment."

Audrey asked him to go with her to an evangelistic crusade, and reluctantly he attended. He admits the message gave him more food for thought, but he didn't raise his hand or go forward during the altar call. He had determined in his mind not to respond to the "emotionalism" of the meeting.

But in the days that followed, little else occupied his mind. "God was after me and was very patient. I knew I had a choice to make, and He brought me to the place of decision at the foot of the cross. I could accept or reject Him, and I knew that making no decision constituted rejection, but I was still stubborn, putting God off. I would choose the time and the place.

"Finally I did just that. I made an appointment with God, and at 8:30 p.m. on Sunday, December 1, 1963, God kept that appointment with me. I confessed my sin and told Him I believed in Christ through reading His Word, the Bible. I asked Him to change my life and help me to live as I ought to."

For a couple of days Bill didn't tell anyone. He became upset that no one noticed a change in him. It was only when he told Audrey about his decision that change began. "The following day I was not looking for someone to notice a change in me. The transformation had begun, and I was the first person to notice it… Half of my vocabulary was eliminated, my drinking stopped, my way of doing business changed. Activities, attitudes, thoughts, and desires were all transformed. I could hardly wait to get to church…

"This was the beginning of my new life. I knew I was 'born again,' a member of God's family, called out of darkness into His marvellous light. I looked forward to each succeeding day and was living proof that '*if any man be in Christ, he is a new creature: old things are passed away; behold, all things are become new.*'"[141]

Bill's story is a beautiful picture of the way the Father pursues us in love and longs for us to come home. The moment Bill believed in Jesus' death and resurrection, all his doubts vanished. The words of Jesus in the Bible spoke truth to Bill's mind, and the Holy Spirit gave him understanding in his heart. God knew exactly what Bill needed and confronted him personally. All the proof was found in Jesus.

---

[141] 2 Corinthians 5:17, KJV.

I'm sharing Bill's story because he's my dad, and I can verify that everything in his testimony is true. I was a teenager at the time, and our family was turned upside down by my father's conversion.

DECONSTRUCTING BELIEF AND FAITH

What is it that takes us from the place of doubt and not knowing God to that place of certainty in who He is and what He has done? A lot of people would say that it's faith, but when Jesus spoke to Thomas He specifically used the word *believe*. "*Thomas, because you have seen Me, you have believed. Blessed are those who have not seen and yet have believed.*"[142]

We often use these two words, *faith* and *believe*, interchangeably, and I suppose having faith and believing are similar, but are they the same? Years ago I had a co-worker who would persistently ask the same question in our team meetings: "What do you mean by that?" Although it was annoying at times, it it showed me how different people define words in different ways. If the meaning I attach to a word is different than the meaning it has for you, there can be confusion and disagreement.

Although these words (*faith* and *believe*) come from the same root in the Greek language (*pistis/pisteuo*), our use of them in English does reveal subtle differences. We all have faith in one thing or another because the activities of life are faith-filled. I have faith in the order and design of the universe and the unchanging laws of nature. I have faith that the water from my tap won't kill me, and even when I sit on a chair I'm demonstrating faith. It's the way I express trust and confidence in the things I accept as reliable.

But faith is quantitative. I can have great faith, or I can have little faith. Faith can help me to find God, but faith doesn't save me. Most people have enough faith to believe that God exists, but the Bible tells us that even the demons know that God exists, and it makes them tremble.[143]

In times of crisis people call out to God for help, even if they don't normally practice or claim any religious affiliation. God has put a sense

---

[142] John 20:29.
[143] James 2:19.

of His reality within our hearts because He doesn't want anyone to be lost.[144] Faith can result in salvation but it is God's love and goodness that brings you to repentance. It is God alone who saves you by His grace because He loves you.

> *For by grace you have been saved through faith, and that not of yourselves; it is the gift of God.*[145]
>
> *Though now you do not see Him [Jesus], yet believing, you rejoice with joy inexpressible and full of glory, receiving the end of your faith—the salvation of your souls.*[146]

Belief, on the other hand, is more specific. You either believe or you don't believe. When you believe something it's because you've processed the facts in your mind, considered the source, and reached a conclusion. The dictionary defines *belief* as "the acceptance of a thing as true."[147] When you accept something as true, you believe in it. When Thomas saw and touched Jesus, he believed. When my dad believed in Jesus, it was more than just an acknowledgment that Jesus had lived and died on a cross. He came to accept as true what the Bible teaches about the death and resurrection of Jesus Christ. Here's what he read:

> *For God so loved the world that He gave His only begotten Son, that whoever believes in Him should not perish but have everlasting life.*[148]
>
> *"For if you do not believe that I am He [the Messiah], you will die in your sins."*[149]
>
> *For the wages of sin is death, but the gift of God is eternal life in Christ Jesus our Lord.*[150]

---

[144] 2 Peter 3:9.

[145] Ephesians 2:8–9.

[146] 1 Peter 1:8–9.

[147] Dorothy Mackenzie, comp., *Oxford School Dictionary*, 2nd edition (London, UK: Oxford University Press, 1960), s.v. "belief."

[148] John 3:16.

[149] John 8:24.

[150] Romans 6:23.

In Him [Jesus] we have redemption through His blood, the forgiveness of sins, according to the riches of His grace.[151]

Dad believed that his sin condemned him and that he was helpless to save himself. When he believed in Jesus he received the forgiveness for which Jesus died and became a member of God's family. The seed of faith that brought him to that moment of decision began to flourish and became the faith that he lived by.

The apostle Paul describes it this way: *"I am not ashamed of the gospel of Christ, for it is the power of God to salvation for everyone who believes."*[152] *"The life which I now live in the flesh I live by faith in the Son of God, who loved me and gave Himself for me."*[153]

A FATHER WHO WATCHES AND WAITS

More than any other story in the Bible, the parable of the prodigal son illustrates our journey home to the Father.

This story begins with a young son asking his father to give him his inheritance. After receiving the money, he leaves home and squanders it on parties and prostitutes, until everything is gone and he finds himself destitute, hungry, and homeless. He ends up slopping pigs as a hired hand, and this is where we'll pick the story up:

"But when he came to himself, he said, 'How many of my father's hired servants have bread enough and to spare, and I perish with hunger! I will arise and go to my father…' And he arose and came to his father. But when he was still a great way off, his father saw him and had compassion, and ran and fell on his neck and kissed him. And the son said to him, 'Father, I have sinned against heaven and in your sight, and am no longer worthy to be called your son.' But the father said to his servants, 'Bring out the best robe and put it on him, and put a ring on his hand and sandals on his feet. And bring the fatted calf here and kill it, and let us eat and be merry;

---

[151] Ephesians 1:7.
[152] Romans 1:16.
[153] Galatians 2:20.

for this my son was dead and is alive again; he was lost and is found.'"[154]

In our lost and unredeemed state, we demand what we want from God, what we think is our right. We take it and use it in ways that God never intended, and the result can be anything from dissatisfaction to devastation. We can choose to carry on living as slaves to the things of this world, or, as the prodigal did, we can come to our senses and turn back to the Father who longs for us to come home.

One of the reasons Jesus told this story was to help us better understand the heart of God. Jesus showed us that God receives us with love even though we don't deserve it. Like the father in the story, God in Christ bears your shame and takes your punishment on Himself. Through all of your rebellion He patiently waits and watches. And then in that moment when you reach the end of yourself and repent, He rushes to meet you. Before you even speak a word He knows your heart and welcomes you home with gifts. He can hardly wait to begin the celebration. There is great joy in heaven when the lost is found and when the one who was dead receives new life.

At the end of a church service or at an evangelistic meeting there may be a call for people to step out in faith and acknowledge that they have believed and put their faith in Christ. Some raise a hand or walk to the front of the church. Some think they're saved by being baptized or by saying a special prayer, but there is no procedure or method that can ever save anyone. Sometimes, people are looking for a spiritual insurance policy rather than a restored relationship with God. Although these present-day practices can be part of the Christian experience, belief in Jesus goes deeper than any outward response. *"If you confess with your mouth the Lord Jesus and believe in your heart that God has raised Him from the dead, you will be saved. For with the heart one believes unto righteousness."*[155] Believing is a matter of the heart... a humble heart that recognizes who God is... a heart that receives forgiveness... a heart that finds assurance and hope in Jesus.

---

[154] Luke 15:17–24.
[155] Romans 10:9–10.

The circumstances that bring people to the foot of the cross will vary, but one thing is certain. It's impossible to be born again into God's family without believing in Jesus. It's impossible to believe in Jesus and not be touched by the Father's love. The Father waits for you because... *there is joy in heaven when a sinner repents.*

CHAPTER 8
The Family Secret

After the 2010 earthquake in Haiti, the world snapped to attention. Over 150,000 people lost their lives, and over a million were left homeless. International relief efforts were set in motion immediately, and churches in our community were eager to help. By holding a gospel music concert and prayer rally we were able to raise several thousand dollars in one evening.

As the concert drew to a close, one of the leaders stepped forward and announced that we would now go into a time of prayer. As he pointed to a list of prayer requests on the screen he went on to say that we first needed to spend a few minutes confessing our sin. He said, "If we don't ask God to forgive us, He won't hear our prayers." Suddenly the air around me seemed to become electric. It was as if God's speaker volume was on high and my receiver was wide open. "Did you hear what was just said? Are you paying attention?" "Yes, Lord, I heard. But why are you asking me this?" End of transmission. Wow! What was that?! I left that night pondering this extraordinary encounter with God.

I THOUGHT ABOUT THIS EXPERIENCE OFTEN OVER THE NEXT FEW DAYS. AT TIMES I WAS tempted to doubt whether God had really spoken to me, but I knew I didn't imagine it. God was clear. Hearing words and paying attention to what they mean are two different things. The leader had said, "If we don't ask God to forgive us, He won't hear our prayers." But isn't this what the Bible teaches us? Just to make sure I started looking up Bible verses about forgiveness. Here's what I found:

> In Him [Jesus] we have redemption through His blood, the forgiveness of sins, according to the riches of His grace.[156]
>
> And you, being dead in your trespasses and the uncircumcision of your flesh, He has made alive together with Him, having forgiven you all trespasses.[157]
>
> Be kind to one another, tenderhearted, forgiving one another, even as God in Christ forgave you.[158]
>
> I write to you, little children, because your sins are forgiven you for His name's sake.[159]

God had my attention now! The teaching of the apostles in the New Testament is that we are forgiven—past tense. Jesus' death on the cross paid the penalty for all the sins of humanity, but if that's true, why do Christians keep asking God for forgiveness?

I had been a believer since I was a child and had taught Sunday school for over twenty years, and yet I had never taken note of this inconsistency. In all of his letters to the New Testament churches the apostle Paul never once instructed the believers to ask for forgiveness! God had graciously brought to my attention what I now call the best kept family secret in the world. If you believe in Jesus, your sin is forgiven!

FORGIVEN OR NOT FORGIVEN?

God's Kingdom operates within a legal framework, and His forgiveness of man's sin was a legal transaction that took place at the cross.

---

[156] Ephesians 1:7.
[157] Colossians 2:13.
[158] Ephesians 4:32.
[159] 1 John 2:12.

The Israelites were well aware that death was the penalty for transgressing God's law and that without the shedding of blood there was no forgiveness of sin.[160] Jewish priests sacrificed animals on the altar, and the high priest entered the Holy of Holies in the temple once each year to make atonement for the sins of the people. Only blood makes atonement for the soul, because life is in the blood.[161] Jesus said the new covenant between God and man was in His blood, and as He hung on the cross He cried out, "*It is finished!*"[162] The Greek word He used, *tetelestai*, is a legal accounting term signifying that the debt was paid in full. God completely forgave every sin because Christ paid the penalty for every sin. All of your sins were in the future when Jesus died, so all of your sins—past, present, and future—were dealt with at the cross. When you confess you are a sinner and accept that He suffered the death penalty in your place, you receive the forgiveness for which His blood was shed.

Nothing I do can ever initiate forgiveness. No amount of asking or pleading with God to forgive me will save me or make me clean. In fact, asking God to forgive me plants messages in my mind that are contrary to the Word of God. It tells me that there is unforgiven sin in my life, that past sin is forgiven but future sin isn't covered. It suggests that God must decide whether He will forgive me—or not. It implies that Jesus' death was not enough. But the Bible says He died once for all. Asking for forgiveness is like crucifying Jesus over and over because in God's economy blood sacrifice is the only action that results in forgiveness. But God was satisfied at the cross, and there is no further sacrifice to be made for the sins of man.[163]

"Realistically, we only have two choices: 1. accept as fact the complete, unconditional forgiveness that God purchased through the crushing of his Son, or 2. create some system of our own to feel better about our sins."[164] Fellow Christians may tell you to claim your forgiveness or keep short accounts with God but any method we create to deal with sin just becomes a self-imposed law and living under law, whether divine or self-

---

[160] Hebrews 9:22.
[161] Leviticus 17:11.
[162] John 19:30.
[163] Hebrews 10:10–12, 18.
[164] Farley, *The Naked Gospel*, 136.

imposed, always leads to more sin.[165] If I don't believe I'm forgiven I'll inspect, analyze and condemn myself but there is no ritual or procedure or requirement that can bring any more forgiveness than what I already have. If I don't believe I'm forgiven it's not because I need forgiveness; it's because I have a problem with unbelief.

> Many years ago my cousin was admitted to the psychiatric unit at the hospital and was diagnosed with clinical depression. Back then I didn't know very much about mental health problems, and it made me feel uncomfortable. So when his mother asked me to visit him, I made excuses. Then on July 30, 1983, we received a call that Brian had left the hospital, walked out into Kempenfelt Bay, and drowned. I was devastated. I had failed to respond to a loved one's call for help and will never know whether a visit from me might have made a difference.
>
> Guilt and shame plagued me for months until a couple of back-to-back sermons by Pastor Jim Stanley helped me to see that my problem was unbelief. He preached on these words of Jesus: "*Come to Me, all you who labor and are heavy laden, and I will give you rest.*"[166] That's what I needed. Rest from my self-condemnation, relief from the burden I carried. *But how, Lord? Where is this rest to be found?*
>
> I didn't have to wait long for the answer. The following week the pastor spoke from the book of Hebrews. "*And to whom did he swear that they [the Israelites] should never enter his rest...? So we see that they were unable to enter because of unbelief.*"[167] I stopped obsessing over my sin, declared my belief in the gospel, and focused on Jesus. I confessed my sin and thanked God that the blood of Jesus paid my debt. Sin's hold on my mind was broken, and my heart began to heal.

---

[165] Romans 7:5.
[166] Matthew 11:28.
[167] Hebrews 3:18–19, RSV.

Acts of sin are a reality in every believer's life. We live in the flesh, and the flesh and the Spirit are in conflict. What then should you do when you sin? First acknowledge and confess your sin to God. Repent and turn from your sin, and then,

Remember who you are in Christ. Remember that there is no condemnation to those who are in Christ.[168]

Give thanks. Always give thanks that your sin is forgiven and that the blood of Jesus was enough to pay your debt.

Stop what you're doing and act differently. By the power of the indwelling Holy Spirit you can choose to say "no" to sin and turn from it. You can choose to say "yes" to righteousness and honour God.

A NEW WAY OF THINKING

Perhaps at this point some of you are scratching your heads and saying "Yes, but didn't Jesus teach us to ask for forgiveness? And if so, why didn't the apostles teach the same thing?"

The answer is simple. We must always remember that the heart of the gospel is the cross of Jesus Christ. It's the place where God drew the dividing line between His old covenant with Israel and His new covenant with all humanity. Jesus was born and lived under old covenant law,[169] and as He began His public ministry He was clear about two things. He had come to minister to the Jews, the lost sheep of Israel,[170] and He was calling His people to embrace change because their old agreement with God was about to become obsolete.[171] Jesus was challenging His people to repent and rethink their relationship with God because the Kingdom of heaven was at hand.[172]

It was years later when the apostles wrote about life under God's new agreement with mankind. The purpose and context of Jesus' teaching before the cross is very different than that of the apostles after the cross, and so it should be.

---

[168] Romans 8:1.
[169] Galatians 4:4.
[170] Matthew 10:6.
[171] Hebrews 8:13.
[172] Mark 1:15.

In His long and famous Sermon on the Mount Jesus is speaking to multitudes of Jewish people. Over and over again He throws standards at them that the best of them wouldn't be able to keep. To show the futility of trying to live life perfectly under the law He says outrageous things like, if your hand causes you to sin, cut it off.[173] If your eye causes you to sin, pluck it out.[174] Be more righteous than the Pharisees.[175] Be perfect like God.[176] By burying them under the demands of the law Jesus is showing them that no one can keep the law and that permanent forgiveness under the old covenant can never be attained. The law always demands more than they can give. He doesn't want them to try harder. He wants them to give up on the old and open their minds to the new. He's preparing them to receive the good news of the gospel.

Jesus next took aim at the repetitious prayers of hypocrites, but the model He suggests is still part of the old system that condemns. By telling them to say, *"forgive us our debts, as we forgive our debtors,"*[177] He's provoking frustration and despair. As He did earlier in the sermon, He's accentuating the wide chasm that exists between God and man. What an irony that we have taken this old covenant prayer, called it The Lord's Prayer, and made it the most repeated prayer of all time.

Jesus knew that the Jews He was addressing wouldn't get the point He was trying to make, so at the end of the prayer He immediately returned to the issue of forgiveness and went on to say, *"For if you forgive other people when they sin against you, your heavenly Father will also forgive you. But if you do not forgive others their sins, your Father will not forgive your sins."*[178] Before Jesus bought our forgiveness at the cross there was no other way for the Jews to relate to God. Apart from their repeated sacrifices they could only expect forgiveness in the same proportion to which they gave it. Jesus' good news is that God's Kingdom is at hand, and in His Kingdom forgiveness will be about love, not effort and ritual.

---

[173] Matthew 5:30.
[174] Matthew 5:29.
[175] Matthew 5:20.
[176] Matthew 5:48.
[177] Matthew 6:12.
[178] Matthew 6:14–15, NIV.

"This is love: not that we loved God, but that he loved us and sent his Son as an atoning sacrifice for our sins."[179]

Does this mean there's nothing for us to learn from this sermon? Absolutely not! Jesus' words challenge me more today than they did His hearers two thousand years ago. Believers today are able to look back from this side of the cross and understand where Jesus was coming from. Divine forgiveness is the expression of God's unconditional love and compassion toward repentant sinners. Do I believe that my debt was totally paid at the cross? Do I forgive others because I've experienced God's incredible gift of grace in my own life? The message I take from Jesus' teaching is this: When I know the sacrifice that Jesus made for me and I receive His forgiveness, how can I not forgive others?

GUARDING THE TRUTH

Certainly the practice of seeking God's forgiveness is prevalent among those who embrace the Christian faith. If you ask people why they repeatedly ask for God's forgiveness, many will refer to 1 John 1:9: *"If we confess our sin He is faithful and just to forgive us our sin and to cleanse us from all unrighteousness."* This Scripture does appear to place a condition on our forgiveness. If we confess, God forgives.

But if there's something that I as a believer have to do in order to be forgiven, then no other New Testament letter mentions it. Could this be an example of Scripture contradicting Scripture? No! Scripture never contradicts Scripture! If there seems to be contradiction, then we're missing something, and we need to dig deeper to uncover the truth. In this case, context is critical to our understanding. John's letter was written to believers *and unbelievers,* and unless we understand the situation he was addressing we might be tempted to misinterpret what he's saying.

> When the apostle John moved to Ephesus, what he found there concerned him. Greek philosophy, false teaching, and cults were slowly infiltrating the churches. One group in particular, the Gnostics, were contradicting John's teaching

---

[179] 1 John 4:10, NIV.

by saying that God would never take on flesh and that sin was not real, that it didn't matter.

Every morning John rose early to pray for the churches. He asked God to give the believers faith and understanding. He asked God to help the believers identify and stand against heresy, and one day as his prayer time ended he felt prompted by the Holy Spirit to write a letter to the churches in and around Ephesus. He began by reminding them that his teaching carried apostolic authority and was based on his own experience with Jesus. He had personally heard and seen and touched the truth that he taught. He then made it perfectly clear to these mixed groups of believers and unbelievers that "*If we say that we have no sin, we deceive ourselves, and the truth is not in us. If we confess our sins, He is faithful and just to forgive us our sins and to cleanse us from all unrighteousness.*"[180]

In the context of growing heresy within the newly established Christian churches, John is not instructing the believers to continually ask God to forgive them, but rather he is inviting the unbelievers in their midst to embrace the truth of the gospel and receive the forgiveness of sin that is theirs in Christ. Earlier in the same letter John wrote, *"If we walk in the light as He is in the light, we have fellowship with one another, and the blood of Jesus Christ His Son cleanses us from all sin."*[181] If I let my sin (which is forgiven) stand between me and God, I will be burdened and enslaved by it. It will rob me of the joy of intimate relationship with God, of walking with Him and experiencing His Father love in my life. In the story of the prodigal son, the father's forgiveness of his son didn't depend on whether or not his son acknowledged need of it, and it wasn't initiated by his son asking for it. The father forgave his son unilaterally and unconditionally, but it was in the confession of his sinfulness that the son received the forgiveness that the father was waiting to give him. And it was in the freedom of that forgiveness that fellowship with his father was restored.

---

[180] 1 John 1:8–9.
[181] 1 John 1:7.

WHAT ABOUT YOU?

Alexander Pope said, "to err is human, to forgive, divine."[182] There's probably more truth in that statement than we realize. There's always a price to be paid, and God didn't sweep sin under the carpet or turn a blind eye to it. In order to forgive your sin, God did three important things.

First, He sent Jesus to pay the debt that you couldn't pay.

Second, because of the death of Jesus, He cancelled your debt. How would you feel if you woke up tomorrow morning and all your bills and credit cards had been paid off? You'd feel like a heavy weight had been lifted. It would be cause to celebrate, to rejoice.

Third, He wiped the slate clean. This payment was a legal transaction signed in blood, and God finalized it with a promise. "*Their sins and their lawless deeds I will remember no more.*"[183] God gave up His right to punish you, to demand an apology, to be bitter or angry towards you, to get even with you. He gave up His right to ever bring up your sin again. When you confess that you are a sinner and believe in Jesus, the sin issue is over. It's done!

Thousands of books have been written on the benefits and "how to" of forgiveness, but human forgiveness is merely a shadow of divine forgiveness. I struggle to forgive both myself and others because in my flesh I don't want to take the penalty of that sin on myself. I choose not to bear that pain, but "All forgiveness, whether human or divine, is in its very nature substitutional… Jesus substituted Himself for us, bearing His own wrath, His own indignation at our sin. That's what forgiveness cost!"[184] True forgiveness is possible when I choose to bear the penalty and pain of another's sin against me. It's an expression of the love of Christ that I can extend to others because I've experienced it myself. The apostle Peter was one of the first to realize this truth.

> Peter turned his head sharply, startled by the shrill cry of a rooster. As he turned back, his eyes met the eyes of Jesus,

---

[182] Knowles, *The Oxford Dictionary of Quotations,* 584.

[183] Hebrews 8:12.

[184] James Buswell Jr., *A Systematic Theology of Christian Religion* (Grand Rapids, MI: Zondervan, 1962), 2:76.

and in that moment there was a dawning awareness of what had just happened. Through the night he had betrayed his Master, not just once but three times. An invisible blow sickened him, and he needed to get away.

The crowd in the courtyard of the high priest was becoming restless as he pushed his way through them to make his escape. Hours later his nerves still felt raw as he watched the crucifixion from a safe distance. Thank goodness John was there with the women.

He could hardly breathe. Anger, frustration, and sorrow boiled inside of him as he paced the streets of Jerusalem. Late that night he made his way back to where the others were staying. Seeing Mary, he collapsed at her feet, and choking back tears he said, "Jesus told me I would deny Him, and when our eyes met I thought I would die—His eyes…His eyes."

Lightly touching his arm Mary asked him, "Peter, what did you see in His eyes?"

With tears now streaming down his face, Peter answered, "Love, I saw only love."

He felt the gentleness of Mary's hand on his face. "He forgave you, Peter. He forgave you, and now you can do no less."

Forgiveness is a choice because… without choice there is no love.

CHAPTER 9
The Family Tree

HELPING PEOPLE TO DISCOVER AND EXPLORE THEIR FAMILY ANCESTRY HAS BECOME BIG business in the 21st century. Most of us are curious about our family roots and countries of origin because it's these connections that give us a sense of identity.

Within me there is an inherent longing to belong, and my desire for community is God's imprint on my soul. Christianity is not only about our salvation. It's about belonging to a family, God's family.

"Aren't we all God's children?" It was a simple question, and Laura was surprised when I said, "No." Her reasoning was that if we're all descendants of Adam and Eve, then we're all God's children, right? I quickly explained to her that Adam and Eve died spiritually when they disobeyed God and that only people who believe in Jesus are God's children. Unfortunately, she didn't seem convinced, and I must admit I wasn't totally satisfied with the answer myself.

Around the same time, I had begun to work on this chapter and had been wavering on its content. Feelings of frustration and a growing pile of discarded notes were

> staring at me. This usually meant that God was waiting for
> me to stop trying so hard and listen. As I further pondered
> Laura's question I suddenly realized that God was speaking.
> How could I write *The Family Tree*, a book about God getting
> His family back, and not address this important question?

A family tree is a chart that uses a treelike structure with branches spreading upward and outward to demonstrate family relationships. I thought about my own family and how complicated a family tree can become after just three or four generations. It made me wonder what God's family tree might look like! Is the whole human race one big family with God at its head?

After speaking with Laura I realized that finding the answer was going to require further thought and study. Most people have an opinion when asked this question, but an opinion is simply that, an opinion. Any question about God is best answered by God, so to get the answer we need we're going to have to look to God and His Word to provide it.

AREN'T WE ALL GOD'S CHILDREN?

How does God answer this question? How does God describe His relationship with people? I began with a search of the word "children" in *Strong's Concordance*,[185] and what I found surprised me.

There are almost no Old Testament references that use the phrase "children of God." Even the most well-known Old Testament characters are not called children of God. Moses was the servant of the Lord.[186] Abraham was God's friend,[187] and David was "a man after His own heart."[188] The Israelites, God's special treasure among all the people on the earth,[189] are called the children of Israel and sometimes described as an unfaithful wife because of their sin and idolatry.

I went back to the concordance, this time to search out Old Testament references to God as "Father." Perhaps this approach would

---

[185] James Strong, *The Strongest Strong's Exhaustive Concordance*.
[186] Deuteronomy 34:5.
[187] James 2:23.
[188] 1 Samuel 13:14.
[189] Deuteronomy 7:6.

shed more light on the nature of our relationship with God. But again I was surprised. There are many verses that use the word "father" but only in reference to human birth connections, i.e., who begat who. These "father" references are never used to describe God's relationship with the people He created.

I began to understand why the Pharisees and the scribes hated Jesus so much. His constant reference to God as His Father was outrageous to them because it was contrary to their interpretation of the Old Testament Scriptures. The only "father" figure in the Jewish religion was Abraham, the great patriarch of the Jewish family. In the Old Testament God never refers to Himself as the Father of Adam or the Father of Israel or the Father of mankind. In describing His relationship with man, God says He is our Maker, our Creator, and our King. He is the Lord God Almighty.

God created the earth to be a home for mankind, an extension of His heavenly Kingdom, but in an act of guerilla warfare Satan seized control of it. In response to this God called Abraham and through him created a family line, which grew to become the nation of Israel. In a legal and binding covenant, Israel agreed to be God's representative on earth and He became their King. But despite all God's effort, the covenant failed.

One day in a heartfelt discussion with the prophet Samuel, God said, *"They have not rejected you, but they have rejected Me, that I should not reign over them."*[190] Due to man's sin and rebellion a personal relationship with God was not possible, and God grieved this loss.[191]

It seemed like all was lost, but then, in the midst of this hopelessness and despair, the Jewish prophets began to speak about a Saviour, a Deliverer. The prophet Hosea said of Israel, *"In the place where it was said to them, 'You are not my people.' there it shall be said to them, 'You are sons of the living God.'"*[192] How could the people of Israel, who were so often estranged from God, suddenly become sons of the living God? The prophet Malachi tells of a Messiah and of a messenger who will

---

[190] 1 Samuel 8:7.

[191] Genesis 6:6.

[192] Hosea 1:10.

announce His arrival,[193] but in the 400 years that follow this prophecy there is no new word from God. It is a time of silence.

Four hundred years is a long time to wait, but if we look more closely we can see that a lot was going on. God may have been silent, but He was not sleeping. God was busy "staging" the earth and making final preparations for the arrival of His Son. During this period the world was dominated by successive empires, including the Persians, the Greeks, and then, finally, the Romans.

Greek rule brought an interest in the arts and fostered a love of literature. The Septuagint (250 BC) was an early translation of the Hebrew Scriptures into the Greek language. Koine Greek became the language of the common man and would become the language of the New Testament. The Roman interest in government and infrastructure led to the construction of an extensive network of roads throughout the Roman Empire, roads that would one day carry the gospel message far and wide. It was only when everything was ready and just as it needed to be that Jesus came.

FIRST CHRISTMAS
A Seed came forth.
The Seed of a woman.
It was not the seed of man
for man's seed can only bring forth mankind.

Alone in the quiet darkness
of the woman's womb
the tiny seed waited.
Suddenly the power of life from on high,
breaking through, becoming one with the Seed.
God had taken on flesh.

He left the glory and the presence of His Father
to dwell in time and space.
And now He waited.
The One who had created the universe

---

[193] Malachi 3:1.

waited within the tiny womb of a woman—
the fullness of time had come.

Breaking forth He cried out
as the cold world gave Him entrance.
Wrapped in cloth and held in arms of love,
He loved the woman back.
She had given Him life
and one day He would give His life for her.

The King of Glory confined to a body
that had been prepared for Him,
while angels sang praises to God
and shepherds bowed in worship.
He was born to die,
but for now He would sleep.[194]

OF MAN OR OF GOD?

All human beings are the descendants of Adam and Eve because we are all made of the same substance. We are all flesh and blood, and our life is in the blood. Adam named the woman "Eve" because she would be "*the mother of all living*,"[195] but when Adam and Eve sinned, the curse of death destroyed God's family. The Spirit of God withdrew from them, and their death was final and complete, spiritually and physically. They became mortal, and the children born to them would bear their image, not the image of God.

Each of us is a one-of-a-kind creation of God with the unique DNA to prove it, but we are not born of God. We are born of man. Whether you are tracking ancestors or descendants, the one element that's common to all family trees is the demonstration of bloodlines. Family trees are about mothers and fathers and the children who are born to them. It's our birth that determines our identity.

---

[194] "First Christmas," Jeanne Best, *The Poetry Collection of Jeanne Best* (December 2015, unpublished).
[195] Genesis 3:20.

I hate it when I fall prey to television advertising. Ancestry.com's advertising campaign is both enticing and persuasive, and I eventually caved in. I ordered the kit, spit in the test tube, and sent my DNA off to be analyzed.

They tell you to be prepared for surprises because the markers that they examine go back hundreds of years. Every time a child is born they carry the unique blend of their parents' DNA. I already had a good idea where my ancestors came from, so I was more interested to see how accurate the analysis would be.

I have to admit, they passed the test! My ancestry was reported to be 100 percent European, with lines to Germany, Great Britain, and Ireland. Ancestry.com has defined what they call seven "countries of origin," but because their analysis is only based on the past few hundred years, it has a limited scope.

If my ancestors were tracked further back in history than Germany, Great Britain, and Ireland, the number of countries and the world's population would become progressively smaller. This tells me that technically we should be able to trace all family lines back to a first man and a first woman, even though we lack the information to actually do so.

If our identity is determined by our birth, then the only way for any of us to become children of God is to be "born again," and this is exactly what Jesus told Nicodemus. *"Unless one is born again, he cannot see the kingdom of God… That which is born of the flesh is flesh, and that which is born of the Spirit is spirit."*[196]

There are no rules we have to keep. There is no ritual we have to perform. God's requirement for membership in His family is very specific. *"As many as received Him [Jesus], to them He gave the right to become children of God, to those who believe in His name: who were born, not of blood, nor of the will of the flesh, nor of the will of man, but of God."*[197]

---

[196] John 3:3–6.
[197] John 1:12–13.

Physically, we can't change our DNA, but in Christ Jesus, God has made provision for us to change our spiritual identity in a real and radical way. *"For as in Adam all die, even so in Christ all shall be made alive."*[198] God removes our dying spirit and puts the eternal life of His Spirit back into us. *"If anyone does not have the Spirit of Christ, he is not His."*[199] It's only when we are born again that we become members of His family. *"For as many as are led by the Spirit of God, these are sons of God."*[200]

TRUE SONS AND DAUGHTERS

Did you know that the first use of a tree as a graphic representation of family is considered to have its "roots" in Christianity? *The Jesse Tree*, a 15th century painting by Jacques de Besancon, depicts the generations from Jesse of Bethlehem to Jesus Christ. It is based on Isaiah 11:1: *"There shall come forth a Rod from the stem of Jesse, and a Branch shall grow out of his roots."*

Jesse was the father of King David, and the figures in the painting are taken from the names listed in the gospels of Matthew and Luke. We may not be able to create a family tree for the entire human race, but God has given us all the information we need to construct the human family tree of Jesus. Jesus referred to the people of His day as the children of men, not the children of God. He in turn identified with humanity by calling Himself the Son of man. Through His mother, Mary, Jesus was born into a family line that's recorded in the Jewish genealogies. His human ancestry can be traced back to King David, then further back to Abraham, and then all the way back to the first man, Adam.[201]

Jesus was human, but He was also God and had every right to call God His Father. Just as humans are made of the same substance, flesh, and blood, so God the Father, God the Son, and God the Holy Spirit are of the same substance. God is Spirit.[202] The life source of God's children is Jesus, the One who is both fully man and fully God, divine Spirit and human flesh.

---

[198] 1 Corinthians 15:22.
[199] Romans 8:9.
[200] Romans 8:14.
[201] Luke 3:38.
[202] John 4:24.

God's family tree is different than the human family tree of Jesus. With the simplicity of an upright beam and a cross beam, it bears no resemblance to the family trees of man. The family tree of God is the cross, and it clearly portrays the relationship between God and His children. It is only through Jesus that anyone can come to God and become a child of God. Jesus said, *"No one comes to the Father except through Me."*[203] The Son of God became the Son of Man so that the sons of men might become the children of God.

God is always in the details. We see it in creation. We see it in His laws. We see it in His plan for the redemption of man. He doesn't want there to be any confusion about membership in His family. He says that Jesus has become the surety of a better covenant[204] and that those who believe in Jesus have "the right" to become His children. It's a strong statement of legal entitlement.

The old covenant was flawed by man's participation, but the new covenant was flawless because God obligated Himself alone to keep it. *"God sent forth His Son, born of a woman, born under the law, to redeem those who were under the law, that we might receive the adoption as sons."*[205] It's a buyout package in which the Son rescues us so that the Father can adopt us.

> An adoption takes place when one person (or more) assumes parenting responsibilities for another, and in our culture today, the adoptee is usually a child. Years ago when I was working as a paralegal and writing wills, I was always careful to find out whether the children that my clients spoke of were natural-born children, stepchildren, or adopted children. A stepchild cannot be the heir of an estate unless they are specifically named in the will. An adopted child, on the other hand, has all the rights and privileges of a natural-born child. Unlike guardianship, custody, or foster care, adoption is a permanent legal transfer of all parental rights and responsibilities.

[203] John 14:6.
[204] Hebrews 7:22.
[205] Galatians 4:4–5.

In Romans times, infant or child adoption was rare because abandoned or unwanted children were not highly regarded and would be taken as slaves. Adult adoption was the norm in those days. Many of the Roman emperors were adopted as a means of strengthening political ties. Adoption was also used for the protection of one's assets. Roman law actually gave an adopted son a higher status than a natural-born child. When a wealthy land owner adopted a son, the new son received a new name and became an instant heir.

Prior to the cross Jesus was the only one who God ever called His Son, and when Jesus took on flesh, He became the firstborn among many brethren. Adoption implies that we are not born as sons and daughters of God. We are orphans and slaves, but based on an act of God we can become true sons and daughters.

In his letter to the Romans, the apostle Paul tells the Christians that through their adoption they enter into this intimate relationship with God and can now call Him Father. *"You received the Spirit of adoption by whom we cry out 'Abba, Father.'"*[206] Because of the nature of adoption in Roman times, Paul's readers would understand that adoption signified a preferred status that was protected by law. Believing in Christ was going to substantially change their lives. "The notion that we are children of God, His own sons and daughters... is the mainspring of Christian living... Our sonship to God is the apex of creation and the goal of redemption."[207] Our adoption by God makes our new identity in Christ both permanent and legal.

"Aren't we all God's children?" I was anxious to revisit this question with Laura. When we understand what God has done for us, it gives those who believe in Jesus a strong sense of belonging and security. Just because you are a member of the human race doesn't mean you automatically qualify for membership in God's family. Only those who believe in Jesus are born again into the family of God. Only those who believe in Jesus are children of God, and... *this is how God gets His family back.*

---

[206] Romans 8:15.

[207] Keller, *Romans 8–16 for You*, 25.

CHAPTER 10
Family Legacies

IN THE OLD TESTAMENT GOD RECOGNIZED TWO GROUPS OF PEOPLE ON EARTH—JEWS and Gentiles. The Jews are God's chosen people, entrusted with His laws, covenants, and promises, and it was through Abraham and his descendants that the promise of blessing for the whole world was made.

After hundreds of years the promise was fulfilled, and Jesus, the Saviour, was born when the Roman Empire was in power. It was an oppressive regime, violent and immoral. Divorce and prostitution were prevalent, and women were considered inferior, even subhuman. Wealth brought luxury but also boredom. There was peace from war but tyranny over the people, and the rift separating Jews and Gentiles was real and hostile.

Jesus never made any attempt to subvert Roman rulership, but He made it clear that His allegiance was to His Father in heaven and that His work was to do the Father's will. He came to fulfill the Old Testament law and prophecies and to lay down His life as a ransom to free people from sin and death.

Jesus healed the sick with mercy and compassion. He performed miracles with power and authority. He treated women with a kindness and respect that was nothing less than revolutionary. When Jesus stepped into history God made a new covenant with all mankind, and now He recognizes two different groups of people on earth—those who believe in His Son, Jesus Christ, and those who don't.

THE FOUNDATION OF THE WORD

The first people who believed in Jesus were Jews, and the transition to a Christian faith that would include both Jews and Gentiles took time and was not easy. The great irony was that the Jews, God's own people who should have understood and welcomed the news, were the least accepting of it.

Saul of Tarsus was a religious leader among the Jews, a fanatic when it came to Jewish law and traditions. He was consumed with hatred towards those who followed Christ and was bent on their destruction.[208] But God knew He could put Saul's talents to better use, and one day on the road to Damascus Saul had his own personal encounter with Christ.[209] He was transformed and thereafter known as Paul, apostle of Jesus Christ to the Gentiles.

At that time the Jewish believers in Jerusalem were called Nazarenes and were thought to be a sect of Judaism.[210] They believed that Jesus was Israel's Messiah, but they continued to adhere to Jewish teaching. To the unbelieving Jews the Nazarenes were like an abscess that needed to be purged from their midst. They considered Paul to be a ringleader of the sect and a traitor, so it's not surprising that, even years later, riots broke out when Paul returned to Jerusalem with Luke. For his own protection Paul was taken by Roman guard to Caesarea, where he remained in custody for the next two years before appealing to Caesar and being moved to Rome. By this time Paul had completed three missionary journeys. He had preached the gospel of Jesus Christ to the Gentiles and had established churches throughout Asia and on into Greece, but by AD 60 Paul found himself under house arrest in Rome, awaiting his appeal.

---

[208] Acts 9:1.
[209] Acts 9:3–6.
[210] Acts 24:5.

Friends and co-workers had come and gone, and now only Luke, his loyal friend and brother in Christ, remained with him in Rome. Luke was a cultured Greek physician who had a passion for history and the arts. He had recently completed a manuscript on the life and ministry of Jesus, and today he was meeting with Paul to discuss his friend's work among the Gentiles.

Luke never tired of hearing Paul's testimony and asked him once again, "Tell me about your experience on the road to Damascus."

"Yes," said Paul, "the whole course of my life changed that day."

> "I heard a voice speaking to me and saying in the Hebrew language, 'Saul, Saul, why are you persecuting Me?…' So I said, 'Who are You, Lord?' And He said, 'I am Jesus, whom you are persecuting… I now send you, to open their eyes, in order to turn them from darkness to light, and from the power of Satan to God, that they may receive forgiveness of sins and an inheritance among those who are sanctified by faith in Me.'"[211]

Paul smiled as he watched his friend taking down notes. "Luke, I've ministered faithfully to the Gentiles and done all that Jesus asked of me, but I still long to see the salvation of my people, Israel. I always went to the synagogue first, but more often than not they drove me out, and sometimes they even beat me. I can only pray for them now. The churches are growing and need so much teaching. I'm confined here for now, but I know that God will use what we write for His glory. The letters I write will give them the instruction they need, and the history you write will tell the world what God has done."

---

[211] Acts 26:14–18.

We can only imagine the discussions that Paul and Luke must have shared. God had gifted both of these men—zealous Jew and Gentile doctor—with a love of writing. God breathed out His Word through them.

The Gospel of Luke, the Acts of the Apostles, and the epistles of Paul to the churches form a major portion of the New Testament. If we just read these Scriptures and don't take time to study their history and background, we miss the wonder of God at work. The outcome of this most unlikely friendship was a permanent written record for the generations that would follow. Through His Word, God has given us everything we need to know about life and family. The Bible is a living legacy to be treasured.

THE FELLOWSHIP OF BELIEVERS

It was difficult for the first Jewish believers to understand that everyone who believed in Jesus was part of God's family, but Peter's testimony about the work of the Holy Spirit in the house of Cornelius, a Roman centurion,[212] finally persuaded the church leaders at Jerusalem that the gospel was for Jews and Gentiles alike.

The apostle Paul shared this same message with the Gentiles:

> *For through Him we both [Jews and Gentiles] have access by one Spirit to the Father. Now, therefore, you are no longer strangers and foreigners, but fellow citizens with the saints and members of the household of God.*[213]

Amidst all the cultural and religious conflict of those early days the Christian church slowly became a unity of believers "*out of every tribe and tongue and people and nation.*"[214] As it grew, the church came to embrace the truth that "*There is neither Jew nor Greek, there is neither slave nor free, there is neither male nor female; for you are all one in Christ Jesus.*"[215]

---

[212] Acts 10–11.
[213] Ephesians 2:18–19.
[214] Revelation 5:9.
[215] Galatians 3:28.

Luke remained in Jerusalem for the two years that Paul was imprisoned at Caesarea, and it was during those turbulent days that the Holy Spirit compelled him to write "*an orderly account*"[216] of Jesus' life and ministry. Being a Gentile from Greece, Luke had little knowledge of Jewish heritage or of the events surrounding the birth of Jesus, but his extended stay in the holy city gave him the opportunity to speak with people like Mary, the mother of Jesus, and James, the brother of Jesus.

Since the crucifixion of her son, Mary had been living at the home of the apostle John, and James had become the head of the church in Jerusalem. Luke's writings reflect the personal testimonies of them and of others who lived and ministered with Jesus. The details recorded in the Gospel of Luke show that those who were interviewed trusted him and understood the importance of his work.

> Luke had waited a long time for this day to come. He had researched the Jewish Scriptures, genealogies, and prophesies. He had interviewed more witnesses than he could count, but part of the story was still missing. He wanted to know more about the birth of Jesus, and there was only one person who could provide that for him. After all these years he was finally going to meet with Mary, the mother of his Lord.
>
> His heart pounded with anticipation as he knocked lightly on the rough timber frame. He was a Gentile. She was a Jew. But as Mary opened the door and greeted him, he was immediately put at ease. There was that instant kinship that the Christian brothers and sisters share, and he knew that this time with her was a divine appointment.
>
> Mary still marvelled that God had chosen her to be the mother of His Son, and, even though she had told the story over and over, Luke could see that the wonder of it all was just as real to her now as it had been then. She spoke of visiting angels and the gentle curiosity of shepherds, but

---

[216] Luke 1:3.

Luke probed deeper. "Tell me what it was like before Jesus was born."

Mary openly shared with him details that only she knew. As she reflected back on the prophetic word that her cousin Elizabeth had spoken over her, the joy of all that God had accomplished suddenly overwhelmed her, and she burst out in praise.

> "My soul magnifies the Lord, and my spirit has rejoiced in God my Savior... For He who is mighty has done great things for me, and holy is His name. And His mercy is on those who fear Him from generation to generation... He has put down the mighty from their thrones, and exalted the lowly... He has helped His servant Israel, in remembrance of His mercy, as he spoke to our fathers, to Abraham and to his seed forever."[217]

Mary and Luke shared a moment of silent worship, and then Mary continued on with the story.[218]

During his stay in Jerusalem, Luke became part of the family of believers there, who shared their possessions, broke bread together, and served the Lord. How limited our knowledge would be without Luke's perspective and description of those days and events! This fellowship was the legacy of love and unity that Jesus gave to His church. *"That you love one another; as I have loved you... By this all will know that you are My disciples, if you have love for one another."*[219] Nowhere else is the power of God's love more clearly portrayed than in the parable of the prodigal son, and Luke is the only Gospel writer who records this moving story about family relationships, coming home, and what it means to belong.

---

[217] Luke 1:46–55.

[218] Note: the words of Mary that Luke quotes appear to the author to be those of an older, wiser Mary rather than a very young Jewish girl. The author challenges readers to consider the context versus traditional interpretation.

[219] John 13:34–35.

THE FESTIVE CELEBRATION

The prodigal son was dead. Not actually, but in the Jewish culture of Jesus' time, any child who treated their parent with this kind of disrespect would have been regarded as dead. The family would have had a funeral. The town's people would have been outraged and disgusted. I'm sure the crowd who gathered to hear Jesus tell the story[220] were wondering what was going to happen next when the boy turned his feet in the direction of home.

He had humiliated himself and disgraced his father. Rejection by his town and his family was pretty much a sure thing, but he had nothing more to lose. His pride was gone. He was broken. Throwing himself on the mercy of his father was all he had left, and the closer he got to home, the more his anxiety grew.

Several times he tried to talk himself out of this pilgrimage. He knew the town's people might stone him for the disgrace he had brought to the family. Jewish law required it. But it didn't matter anymore, because he was going to die anyway. His life as he had known it was over. He knew that he was dead to his father, and there was no punishment worse than the life he now lived.

The sight of his father in the distance filled him with a sick dread, but something told him to keep going. As his father approached, the boy collapsed on the ground at his feet. Bracing himself for a tirade of angry words or a beating, he was unprepared for what happened next.

His father fell on him and kissed him. This display of unconditional love was so unexpected that he momentarily pulled back. "No, Father, I have sinned against heaven and against you and am no longer worthy to be called your son."

But before he could continue his father interrupted and called for gifts to be brought. The young man couldn't believe it! His father had forgiven him!

---

[220] Luke 15:11–32.

Can you imagine the relief and gratitude that must have filled the young man's heart? He was unworthy and undeserving of the compassion shown to him, and yet he had been given a second chance.

It's interesting that the father doesn't wait until they're back at the homestead before he brings out the gifts. He doesn't hold off until later when the party is in full swing. It's in that moment when the prodigal bows in humility and acknowledges his sin that he receives the forgiveness his father has been waiting to give him.

As they embrace, the boy's father calls the servants to bring sandals, a robe, and a ring. These particular gifts were powerful cultural symbols showing that this "dead" young man had been fully reinstated as a son and an heir. God shows us that His response to sinners is immediate, extravagant, and undeserved.

Father and son are reconciled, but it is only when the young man receives his father's gifts that he is ready to take part in the celebration already underway at home. Likewise, God the Father has gifts for those who humbly acknowledge their sin. When you believe in Jesus you receive the forgiveness that God has been waiting to give you. He makes you clean and righteous and restores life in you.[221]

It reminds me of an ad for dish detergent in which a little duckling, covered in greasy black oil, is rescued from an oil spill. Gentle hands wash the little duck, freeing it to be all that it was created to be. Jesus took the greasy black oil of your sin on Himself and died in your place. But you're only ready to enter into the celebration when you're dressed for the occasion.

Heaven rejoices every time another child is adopted into the family, and these gifts of forgiveness, life, and righteousness are your party clothes. They're a family legacy.

THE FATHER'S JOY

Despite the joy and celebration, there is a second part to the parable. The father of the estate has another son, and upon his arrival home at the end of the day, the story takes a dramatic turn.

When I was growing up, the sermons I heard on the parable of the prodigal son gave me the impression that the prodigal represented sinners

---

[221] Romans 5:17; 2 Corinthians 5:21.

and that the older "good" son represented believers. The message was that believers needed to forgive those who had offended them. But now as I study the parable I believe Jesus intended a different interpretation.

Jesus was speaking to an audience of scribes and Pharisees as well as tax collectors and sinners. He introduced His story by saying, *"A certain man had two sons,"*[222] and as the tale of these two sons progresses we see that Jesus was targeting those who had come to hear Him. The two sons represent the two groups of people in His audience and how they each respond to Him in very different ways.

Like the tax collectors and sinners, the prodigal had a self-indulgent lust that led to an immoral lifestyle. He became a rebel and an outcast with little concern for what others thought. Only when he came to the end of himself was he able to receive what he didn't deserve. His older brother, on the other hand, hid his sin and denied his guilt. Like the Pharisees with their religious hypocrisy, he deceived himself with self-righteous thoughts. He believed that his goodness and service counted for something. He believed that he'd earned what didn't belong to him, and all the while he was boiling with anger and resentment. He was as hopelessly lost as his prodigal brother was. He just wouldn't admit it.

Jesus' message is that all of us are sinners in need of the Father's love and forgiveness. The father who runs to receive his prodigal home is the same father who leaves the joyous celebration to meet with his other boy in the dark of night. The atmosphere is tense as the father expresses love for this one, who has firmly planted his feet outside and refuses to join the party. The father loves even when he isn't loved in return, and the story stirs us because at some level we identify with these characters and their emotions. Jesus was good at doing that.

But then the story ends abruptly, and Jesus leaves a silent question hanging in the air: Will you enter in or remain outside? Will you believe in Me or reject Me?

The Family Tree is about God's persistent call for lost souls to come home. It's about a love we will never fully understand, the forgiveness we don't deserve, and "the tortuous lengths to which God will go to bring

---

[222] Luke 15:11.

His family home."[223] The Father's desire is to share Himself with us and to extend His Heavenly Kingdom through us. And it is to this end that He pursues us.

The anticipation of believers today will soon be tomorrow's huge family reunion in the Kingdom of God, but that will just be the beginning of the celebration. The sons and daughters of God will one day rule with Him beyond the barriers of time and space in a reality that explodes with His glory. It's the Father's joy for those who believe in Jesus to share in His inheritance, the glorious legacy of eternal life and love that's prepared for all His children.

The only question that remains is this: Have you entered in, or are you still outside? Whether or not you believe in Jesus is a choice for you to make because... *without choice, there is no love.*

---

[223] Yancey, *Vanishing Grace*, 51.

YOU'RE INVITED

"If we confess our sins, He is faithful and just to forgive us our sins and to cleanse us from all unrighteousness" (1 John 1:9). The Holy Spirit of God convicts us of our sin. He calls us to repentance, and then the Father patiently waits. This is your invitation to come home and celebrate all that Jesus has done for you.

> Father God,
>   I come to You with a humble heart, recognizing my sin and rebellion against You. Thank You for sending Jesus to take the punishment that I deserved. I believe He died on the cross and shed His blood for me. I believe that He rose from the dead in power and that I am forgiven. Lord, I trust You and surrender my life to You.
>
> Signed _____

Welcome to the family of God!

Tell someone about your decision, and find friendship with other Christians. Read God's Word, and let Him speak to you through it. Talk to Him and thank Him for all He's done. Watch to see where He's working, and then go and join Him. He loves you, and you are His!

Bibliography

Arthur, Kay. *Our Covenant God.* Colorado Springs, CO: Waterbrook Press, 1999.

Buswell Jr., James. *A Systematic Theology of Christian Religion.* Grand Rapids, MI: Zondervan, 1962.

Colson, Charles. *The Problem of Evil.* Wheaton, IL: Tyndale House, 1999.

Farley, Andrew. *The Naked Gospel.* Grand Rapids, MI: Zondervan, 2009.

Keller, Timothy. *Romans 8–16 for You.* N.p.: The Good Book Company, 2015.

Lewis, C. S. *Mere Christianity.* New York, NY: Macmillan-Collier, 1960.

Lutzer, Erwin. *The Serpent of Paradise.* Chicago, IL: Moody Press, 1996.

MacArthur, John. *A Tale of Two Sons.* Nashville, TN: Thomas Nelson, 2008.

McGee, Robert. *The Search for Significance.* Nashville, TN: Thomas Nelson, 2003.

Murray, Andrew. *The Two Covenants.* Fort Washington, PA: Christian Literature Crusade, 1995.

Sanford, John. *Transformation of the Inner Man.* Plainfield, NJ: Bridge Publishing, 1982.

Smith, John E., Harry S. Stout, and Kenneth P. Minkema, eds. *Jonathan Edwards Reader.* New Haven, CT: Yale University Press, 2003.

Strong, James. *The Strongest Strong's Exhaustive Concordance.* Grand Rapids, MI: Zondervan, 2001.

Yancey, Philip. *Vanishing Grace.* Grand Rapids, MI: Zondervan, 2014.